ADVANCE PRAISE

Bryan Miles has been a mentor and key advisor to my rapidly growing business. He gets people, leadership, and entrepreneurialism, and he is a master on how work gets done in today's crazy environment. Virtual Culture is a must read if you want to experience transformative results in any of those areas.

—MIKE WEINBERG, TWO-TIME BEST-SELLING AUTHOR, CONSULTANT, SPEAKER & CHIEF SALES COACH

Bryan Miles is a leader's leader. He has a gift of seeing the future before most people even figure out what's happening today. Even better, he acts on it. Read this and get ready.

—CAREY NIEUWHOF, AUTHOR AND FOUNDING PASTOR, CONNEXUS CHURCH

Bryan will continue to pave the way for virtual workforce solutions. As a customer and friend, I can assure you that you won't find anyone better.

—MATT LOWE, SWIFT STRAW

Virtual culture isn't just theory for Bryan. He has masterfully created it. If you want to know what the future looks like from the bow of the ship, this book is a must read.

Bryan Miles is a leader with incredible foresight. He has led his team to new ways of thinking and working with extraordinary results. He's disrupting our traditional paradigms and leading us to discover new ways of leading. If you're brave enough to follow his wisdom, your organization will not just survive but thrive in today's culture.

Bryan is a leader full of courage, faith, and integrity who doesn't just lead a great organization, but leads great people who make up a great organization. From his company's inception, I have watched Bryan forge a new path in this space that inspires me to dream bigger and work harder in my own field.

Bryan has not just built a company; he's created an industry. His vision, innovation, and commitment to building a great place to work have been an invaluable resource to me, and it will be for you, too. Pick up Virtual Culture today. You won't regret it!

Over the last decade, I've been a customer, colleague, and friend of Bryan's, and he always brings integrity and leadership to each relationship. These days, anybody can write a book, but few people can build a company culture like he has. It's truly unbelievable. I wouldn't work for many people, but I would be happy to be under his leadership. I can't wait to buy a case of his books.

—CASEY GRAHAM

Bryan is an innovative, straightforward, and creative leader with a contagious passion for virtual services, and he practices what he preaches. He is leading the way to a more productive and flexible workplace!

—CHRIS FOWLER, CHURCH COMMUNITY BUILDER

The more I get to know Bryan, the more I learn of his genuine love for people and his unrelenting desire to challenge the status quo. He inspires greatness by constantly refusing mediocrity in how we work, how we connect, and how we do life.

—HRISHI BASKARAN, HRISHI BASKARAN COMPANY, LLC, A MEMBER OF TABLE GROUP CONSULTING

VIRTUAL CULTURE

VIRTUAL CULTURE

THE WAY WE WORK
DOESN'T WORK ANYMORE

A MANIFESTO

BRYAN MILES

LIONCREST
PUBLISHING

VIRTUAL CULTURE

The Way We Work Doesn't Work Anymore, a Manifesto

ISBN   978-1-61961-721-6 *Paperback*

978-1-61961-722-3 *Ebook*

CONTENTS

———

FOREWORD

BY TED KINGSBERY,
PRESIDENT OF THE
SHARK GROUP

———

You know those moments when you realize you're never going to look at your business the same way again? Well, if you've been lucky enough to experience this, you probably already know that they don't happen very often—and when they do, you need to move immediately on this newfound worldview.

That was exactly how I felt the first time I spoke in depth with Bryan about bringing on a virtual assistant to help with some administrative work that unexpectedly piled up for one of my companies.

I work with Daymond John, one of the stars of the Emmy

Award winning business TV show *Shark Tank*, as the president of his consulting firm the Shark Group. We manage all of his *Shark Tank* investments and his outside investments, and then we consult in various areas such as branding strategy, product development, social media, digital activations and campaigns, celebrity and influencer marketing, retail strategies, and much more. Some of our clients include top brands like Chase, Miller-Coors, and Shopify, as well as some legendary celebrities like Carlos Santana, Catherine Zeta-Jones, and Daymond himself.

When you work with as many companies as we do and help entrepreneurs like our *Shark Tank* partners fortify their operations on a regular basis, the only thing you can expect to happen is the unexpected.

Our team has used virtual assistants in a number of different ways, including:

- Managing customer service centers (especially the night when a company was featured on *Shark Tank*)
- Managing communication like calls, callbacks, emails, etc.
- Scheduling calls and meetings
- Providing research on various topics
- Overseeing projects
- Figuring out random problems that just popped up

To be honest, when I first met Bryan and his wife, Shannon, over four years ago, I wasn't 100 percent sure about it, either. While I had heard great things about Bryan's company, I was cautiously optimistic about hiring a virtual assistant and still doubted whether it would actually work effectively.

Like most leaders, I was thinking, "Will I be able to communicate effectively if I'm not speaking face-to-face with people? Won't the lack of real interaction keep us from working effectively? Maybe it works for other people, but there's no way it will work me. I have unique needs!"

Well, I was wrong. Turns out, my needs weren't that unique.

After my first month of having a virtual assistant with Bryan's company, I knew immediately that all the myths I had heard about were just that.

Not only did my virtual assistant help tackle all of those projects that had piled up, but pretty soon, she looked at our communication techniques and identified ways to streamline everything by consolidating tasks, utilizing the best technology and software for our particular projects, and leaning on her experience of working with many other people with different work habits themselves.

For anyone who is still on the fringe of whether or not this "virtual" or "remote" industry is an effective way of managing responsibilities, efficient with today's technology, or simply just a fad, you'll need to listen to Bryan before you fall behind in the new way business is being done across the globe. Each day, we see more and more organizations opting for a virtual workplace over a traditional office. As a leader, simply put, you can choose to proactively embrace the fact that virtual working is the future of business, or you can just reactively bury your head in the sand. The decision is yours.

For me, I am embracing it.

With the world moving so quickly these days, we all need to have an adapt-or-die mindset. And just like you look around the world and wonder how people functioned before iPhones, the internet, TV, and the radio, future generations will look at us and say the same thing about virtual assistants.

The sooner you realize this massive shift, the sooner you'll get a better sense of the way the world is moving in other areas. Without a doubt, you'll see the reality is that virtual is here to stay.

ACKNOWLEDGEMENTS

(AKA EXPRESSING MY GRATITUDE)

———

Ingratitude sucks! Ingratitude is defined as the state of being ungrateful or unthankful. That is soooooo not me! Spend any time around me, and you'll know I am one of the most grateful people on the planet! When you fail to say thank you, you to fail to close the loop on expressing your appreciation for what others have done for you. In short, ingratitude (aka ungratefulness) is just plain selfish!

Here's the deal. I am insanely grateful to many who had their part, big or small, in helping me achieve this book. I am going to forget someone, but it is not intentional. Just know deep down as I write these acknowledgements, I thank you because this book is the culmination of years of experiences, interactions, and people helping me in my journey. I could not have done it without those who invested in me in many ways.

Okay, here we go!

God, thank you for being my rock and Savior. Thank you for overseeing our business and helping me steward it well with Shannon. Thank you for the opportunities you have afforded me. Thank you for making me and being my friend. Thank you for giving me equal parts wisdom and courage. Thanks for letting me take risks and make decisions that I think you grin at. I hope I am making you proud. I think I am.

Shannon, my Nene...this thing called BELAY and all that it has encompassed over the years with businesses, employees, etc., you've been right there with me...through it all! I'm not only grateful to call you my wife, but also my best friend, my safe place, and my love. Thank you for marrying me half my life ago and for giving us the opportunity to raise each other. Thank you for encouraging me to write this book. I love you so much!

Rainey and Harper...much of what I do is for you. In so many ways, you make me a better man and dad. I love how you are growing up and enjoying life! You make me laugh, enjoy life, and be present. You're amazing kids, and I am sooooo proud of each of you!

Our moms...thank you for all that you have done to help us with our kids and supporting us with your love and encouragement. We love you.

Paige...thank you for laughing at my stupid jokes and representing me so well over the past five-plus years! You are a great work-alongside partner, and you always do a great job to represent me so well, regardless of the task at hand! I am proud to be your boss because you are an excellent leader, human being, assistant, mom, wife, friend, and so much more.

Tricia...thank you for being my first virtual assistant (albeit way overqualified) and for being an amazing leader! It's a sheer joy to watch you lead our team at BELAY! You are a great person on so many levels. Thank you for being with Shannon and me almost from minute one!

LZ...thank you for your passion and dedication to our business. Your heart shines through, and I know we can count on you in many ways. Thank you for your leadership and oversight, especially with our finances and culture! You have filled those big shoes quite nicely!

Our Lead Team (Amy, Jen, Krisha, and Lori)...I can't think of a stronger group of leaders to jump in a foxhole and fight with! You four are great leaders in your disciplines, and it is a joy to do leadership at BELAY with each of you!

Corporate Team...you all rock! Not only does each of you perform so well from your homes every day and knock it out of the park, but you also have collectively had a hand in this book and have served as an example to other organizations. Each day, when you show up and are awesome, you are creating something special: a living, thriving, virtual culture producing amazing results! This book would not happen without you! Grateful to each of you!

Contractors...simply put, thank you for showing up and serving our clients so well! Each day, we rely so heavily on each of you! You work with such heart and care! You've helped us turn heads in our industry by just serving each client the same way you would want to be served! We would not have a business without you! Thank you, thank you, thank you!

Clients...thank you for being brave and for selecting BELAY to help you scale to new heights with your organization. It brings me sheer pleasure to serve leaders and companies like you with our services! Keep changing the world and making it a better place, and we'll be there to help you behind the scenes! We are cheering you all on! BELAY on!

Dr. Thom Rainer...thank you for letting us highlight Life-Way in this book to illustrate your reinvention with a more remote and virtual company! Not only are you providing an epic example of how a very large organization with five-thousand-plus employees can go "remote," but you're also enhancing and preparing your organization for its next set of challenges and opportunities! You are an amazing leader to learn from, and I am proud to call you a friend.

Jeff Hussey...your lovingly blunt words over the years have been so impactful on my life and that of my family. Your encouragement and safe harbor have been so needed. I can't begin to thank you enough for your advice, and even some I didn't ask for. You are a great example of a human being and friend.

Jeff Maness...man, I love your heart and passion for your church, Wyoming, and God! It is a joy to watch you lead! And thank you for being among the first clients ever for my company. I will never forget our first meeting in early December 2010 where I shared with you the idea of a virtual assistant. Thank you for taking a risk on me! I will never forget it!

Michael Hyatt...thank you for being one of the best advocates for our company! In a lot of ways, you are our Oprah, and you've put us on the radar in a big way, and I am forever thankful! You and Gail are the real deal and an amazing example. It has been a joy to serve you and your team over the years.

Richard Chancy...who else on the earth will put up with my CEO Sabbaticals like you?! I am grateful to have a great friend like you. From running steps on the London Bridge in Lake Havasu, climbing Bell Rock in Sedona, watching you almost die eating jalapeno poppers, backpacking in the Wind River Range, or knocking snow off our tents in the Tetons, I can count on you not only for great conversation, but for your wit. Grateful for you, Buddy. You're an example to so many. It's an honor to call you friend!

Casey Graham...thank you for partnering with Shannon and me in the early days of MAG Bookkeeping. You are the consummate serial entrepreneur, and I really love watching you start new things! Thanks for always being real and creating cool new companies!

Bill Couchenour...when I think of the word "leadership," you come to mind instantly. I can't thank you enough for your personal investment in me when you were my boss. You helped me figure out why I wanted to lead others and be in leadership. I can clearly tell anyone my "why" in large part because of you.

Hrishi Baskaran...thank you for leading our Lead Team at BELAY this past year. You single-handedly have redeemed my views on business consultants! Not only have you really invested in our leaders at a personal level, you have also given us some really great tools to grow on. Well done, friend!

Mike Weinberg...just plain thank you for being you! You are an amazing client and friend! Thank you for your encouraging words to me and for helping our sales team! I love our fledgling bromance, and I love the way you punch fear in the throat! Keep slaying it!

Glenn Bryan...words cannot fully articulate how much I appreciate you. In my college days with my dad dying, I had a friend in you. A place where I could safely work out my emotions, thoughts, and dreams. You and Colleen are the best! I still think of many of things you taught me.

Regi Campbell...thank you for challenging me and letting me call you my mentor. Your transparency and words have literally altered my life for the better. I am eternally grateful for you and your example. Thank you for your investment in me.

Jim Underwood (aka our finance savant!)...Shannon and I can't thank you enough for putting up with us and helping us navigate several business challenges that have shown up over the years. Your kind and steady hand is so appreciated. Thank you for being a great example to follow with your faith, family, and profession.

Bill Watkins...man, you are the real deal! You're like a transparent business consultant, überfit grandpa, hiking partner, business networker, company advocate, and close friend all wrapped up in one! Thank you for investing in me and my family in so many ways. You have my permission to speak into my life! Especially helping me circle in on my Zone of Genius. I hope I am the great friend to you that you have been to me!

Ted Kingsbery...thanks for believing in our company and in what we are trying to do with our industry. Thanks for being open-minded and helping BELAY in a lot of ways. I am grateful for your leadership and friendship. You are good people.

The GI! I can't think of another eleven people I'd rather do life with! Thank you for consistently being there for us over the last decade in so many ways! From epic trips to back-porch antics to sad times, great times, limo incidents, ITUBA, parties, and more. My life is just way richer because of you guys!

The Book in a Box team (Coleen, Meghan, Barbara, Elizabeth, and Tucker)...wow! I had no idea how in the world to get these ideas out of my head and into print, and then you guys came along and showed me the way! You guys rock in so many ways! I love your personal touch and encouragement. You have made the work of writing a book a real joy and a great experience! I can't thank you enough, and I love the way you are turning the publishing industry on its head! Keep going!

Most of this book was written under the heavy influence of music. Thank you to the creative genius of U2, the Black Crowes, Snow Patrol, Bruce Hornsby, Blink 182, Explosions in the Sky, Lynyrd Skynyrd, George Michael, Pete Yorn, Coldplay, Beck, Ray LaMontagne, the Zac Brown Band, and Johnny Cash.

INTRODUCTION

TIP OVER THE VIRTUAL WATERCOOLER

———

In 2012, Marissa Mayer left Google Inc. to become the CEO of Yahoo. She was brought in as the turnaround guru for the struggling tech giant, and her plan was to take the playbook that she had used at Google and simply apply it to Yahoo. This game plan included a move to keep her employees in the office for longer periods of time.

For employees in the tech world, working remotely and virtually is not uncommon, but Mayer felt that their physical absence from the office was part of the reason why Yahoo was struggling. She wanted to change that by transforming the Yahoo offices into a place where the employees would want to spend all of their time. Her theory was that if employees wanted to be at work, then their productivity would increase, which would positively affect the bottom line. In part, she was trying to shift the company culture.

Her game plan didn't work.

It was not the saving grace that Yahoo needed.

The corn hole and beer fridges weren't appealing enough to keep her employees away from their work, family, and lives that all took place outside of the office. When she realized that her big plan wasn't delivering the results she hoped for, Mayer brought down the hammer and straight out banned her employees from working from home.

Her decision shocked many. Yahoo was a tech giant—a primary mover in the tech space, which is known for being a progressive industry. But Mayer's act went against that culture. By enforcing that everyone come back into the office, Mayer tried to apply old-school collaboration to a group of people that did not want that style anymore.

You might be able to predict what happened: her employees were not happier and certainly not more productive. Time has shown that Mayer's decision to go against the agile, innovative culture and return to the traditional corporate work environment requiring employees to come to the office and stay there all day was not a good decision.

I suspect that Mayer fell prey to something that many traditional executives or business owners fall prey to: the idea that "If I can't see you, I can't control you. If I can't see you, how do I know that you are working?"

They believe (falsely) that they're not getting the value or the productivity out of their employees. What this thinking shows is that they have no trust in the worker.

By telling their employees they had to be in the office, Mayer and her leadership team were inherently saying that they didn't trust their employees to get their work done without being supervised.

Their actions said to employees, "You're a child. You can't get the job done. Get back into the playpen so we can watch you and make sure you are playing."

So, fully grown adults who were very smart and very capable and very intelligent left Yahoo. Who's shocked by that?

During the height of this blowup, a couple of people in the press called me. They called me because they saw my company, BELAY (which is one of the largest providers of virtual assistants, virtual bookkeepers, virtual webmasters, and virtual content writers in the world), and my values as being the antithesis of Mayer's. They wanted to know what I thought of the ordeal.

I didn't know the intimate details of Yahoo's blunder, but I did know the workforce was demanding greater flexibility in their work environments—even back in 2012. Workers wanted to work from wherever they pleased, whether that was at home, on the road, or in their favorite coffee shop. Most importantly, they wanted their employers to trust that they could get the job done without supervision. I told reporters during this incident that top talent was already moving in that direction, and before long, even more workers would demand that same flexibility from their employers.

I saw the shift happening, and I knew that change was only going to speed up.

If Mayer had looked forward a couple of years when she first mandated her work-from-home ban, then she would have understood just how damaging her mistake was going to be. Tragically, Yahoo was sold to Verizon for $4.8B. At one point, it was valued at over $100B. Mayer's decision to call every employee back in the office wasn't the only reason for their demise.

CULTURE CAN BE PRESENT IN A VIRTUAL WORKFORCE

Mayer, and many like her, subscribe to the old holdout that culture is made by forcing people to sit next to their colleagues in an actual office. Except that isn't how culture is created. Shared vision, not shared spaces, creates a culture. It is about instilling a sense of belonging for your employees and ensuring they identify with the greater mission and values of the company.

And contrary to what Mayer believed, culture can be created without an office. My company is living proof of this. For example, *Entrepreneur Magazine* ranked my company, BELAY, number one in Best Culture for Small-Sized Companies. We've also won Top Company Culture for a Small Business Award for having a "productive" and "high-performance" culture from *Entrepreneur Magazine*.

Additionally, *Inc. Magazine* ranked us as one of the Fastest-Growing Companies in the United States in 2015, 2016, and 2017. We've won a When Work Works Award from the Society of Human Resource Management, an award that recognized "companies that offer effective and flexible workplace strategies, empowering their organization to rise above the competition." And *Atlanta Business Chronicle* named BELAY as one of the "Best Places to Work."

We've won these major culture and business awards from prominent national magazines and outlets despite the fact that not a single one of our team members shares an office. Why? Because we understand how culture is really created. Because we instill our mission and values of gratitude, teamwork, vision, passion, fun, and God into every one of our six-hundred-plus team members.

VIRTUAL WORKS. I'VE LIVED IT.

I've been working remotely in sales since 2001, so I've experienced the merits of being remote and virtual for nearly two decades. Before that, I worked for a publicly traded software dot-bomb. It was awesome because the leaders caught tons of money on fire, and we didn't have to do much. We watched the stock ticker daily with our soon-to-be worthless options, threw crazy sales parties, and pumped the kegs on Beer Fridays. I was in my early twenties, and we mostly hung out in the office and played Ping-Pong all day and drank free Yoohoo. I enjoyed the people I worked with. Mayer would have approved!

Then the bubble burst as fast as it had grown. So, I took a job selling Microsoft solutions for a Canadian Value-Added Reseller and was on the road, up in the air, or working from home most of my time. I got used to working outside of an office, and I found that I loved it. It was freeing. I treasured the autonomy.

After that, I ended up working in sales as a Project Consultant for a construction company that built churches in the US. A few years in, I got promoted to VP of Consulting, and I managed a team of ten sales guys and had my own virtual assistant, Tricia.

To call her an assistant is a disservice because she was a kick-ass, take-no-prisoners executor of all things with an incredible work ethic. She did everything: chasing down subcontractors, holding my sales team in line, overseeing Gantt charts and critical paths, and setting up my dentist appointments. She was able to run my business and personal life, even though she lived four hours away. I was in Atlanta, Georgia; she was in Charlotte, North Carolina. She was able to get her work done for me and get on with her life, and I saw just how happy that made her.

And don't miss this: we didn't need to see each other each day to accomplish the results that were expected of me.

It was my relationship with my then-assistant that sparked in my mind, "Hey, this virtual employee thing is awesome—even better sometimes—for both me as the employer and Tricia as the employee."

At the time, right before I started BELAY, I was traveling like crazy. My kids, Harper and Rainey, were very young. I never got to see them or my wife. I wanted a change so that I wouldn't miss out on their lives. I also had this nagging entrepreneurial itch I couldn't seem to shake. I wanted to build something of my own.

I put two and two together and figured, "If the virtual assistant thing works for Tricia and me, why can't it work for everyone?" I decided to find out and partnered with my wife (who was already very successful in her own career working for a massive corporation) in an effort to bring virtual employee solutions to employers by matching them with virtual employees.

So, after much discussion, research, prayer, and time spent with successful business people asking a bunch of questions, my wife and I cashed out all of our 401(k) s to use as our start-up capital. On October 1, 2010, she gave her sixty-day notice, and I gave my forty-five-day notice. That's right, you read it right, the same day we resigned from our very stable jobs on the heels of the "Great Recession." We wanted to finish out well in case this whole idea didn't work—or, if it did work, we hoped our employees would treat us with the same level of respect one day. December 1, 2010, was our first day on our own company payroll. We went all in on all virtual.

It's been a wild-but-incredibly-successful ride since that day. We've managed to grow a thriving company with an award-winning culture and an entirely virtual workforce. We have no office space—not one square foot of it. We firmly believe working virtually is the future, and I want to bring you and your company along with us into the virtual revolution.

THE JUMP REQUIRES BRAVERY

To see a future where you can grow and maintain a healthy culture all while being virtual takes a certain amount of bravery. It involves venturing into the unknown. Some of the bravest CEOs are the ones who are out there right now throwing around the idea of moving toward a virtual work environment. But many leaders are afraid of doing this because when you strip away the office, you strip away the perception of the company in the traditional mindset.

Many leaders or owners believe the four walls of the office are what keep employees contained within the company. What will happen if you strip away those walls? What is left to keep employees coming back?

For many CEOs, they don't want to find out the answer because they fear the answer is "nothing." Maybe nothing is left to keep employees coming back. This sends a shiver down the spines of many leaders. Did it send one down yours?

The real thing that ultimately keeps employees together is the mission and the act of working together toward something they truly believe in, not a physical office. CEOs must be brave because when they strip away the office, they are taking the gamble that they have created a business whose mission and values are concrete enough to contain and inspire a workforce. That's a pretty big wager for those whose mission is not cutting it.

The decision to go virtual also requires action. Leaders have to communicate with employees about what a virtual workplace means, then provide them with the tools and resources to make it a reality.

I renovated a fast-growing, non-denominational church for a young pastor in Charlotte, North Carolina, who used to say, "You have to say it until you see it."

I thought that was such a smart saying because it is about the importance of vision-casting. If you want to create a certain future for yourself, envision it and talk about it. Leaders often don't do that. The few who do only share that vision with a select few people in leadership, not the entire company. If a CEO is thinking about moving to a virtual workforce, he or she needs to talk about it and vision-cast it so employees will understand what is happening and why.

Once leaders do that, they then need to make sure employees have the appropriate tools to collaborate in a virtual environment. They have to make sure their tools are web-based versus application-based. In other words, they need to enable mobility. Offering mobility is difficult for some enterprises that have relied heavily upon applications that live on hardware and desktops within the office.

On the other side of action is reward. I can't tell you how many lives a virtual work environment can change. One of the women on my leadership team emailed me recently to tell me how jealous all of her friends were that she had found a company like mine that allowed her to work from home, love her job, love the mission, and be able to be a much more present mother to her children. Her daughter is going away to college next year, and her son will soon follow. These are critical years in her children's lives, and she is so happy she can be with her kids and hold a great job and not miss a beat.

Her story proves you can have a thriving corporate life and a rewarding personal life. You don't have to trade the two.

Her story and the many other stories I hear from my employees, clients, and contractors are what make me proud of BELAY and the mission it espouses. I've spoken to countless CEOs and business owners who envy my model. They would love to implement it, they tell me, but they can't figure out how to get there.

This book will help them see that creating a virtual workforce with an enduring culture is possible. This book is my attempt to help them say it before they see it.

Frankly, a virtual workforce is the future. Accenture has predicted that by 2020, 43 percent of the workforce will be freelance; they've dubbed this workforce as a "liquid workforce." Why "liquid"? Because these people will be free. They won't be in a corporate office chained to desks and confined in cubicles. They will move with total autonomy. Millennials are the biggest driver of this change and, since they now take up the bulk of the workforce, they are imposing a lot of pressure.

People of all ages in the workforce see that this type of world is out there—and so do I! They see a future where they can conduct a meeting from their back deck or meet with a client while sitting on their couch. A world where they can contribute, execute, and have flexibility and autonomy all at the same time.

In my experience, anyone who has had the chance to work virtually will never go back. It's hard to convince an employee that a traditional office work environment is great when they've had the opportunity to work off their back deck. My company has ruined going into work for most of our employees and clients; they refuse to return to a traditional workplace.

Who wants to sit in a stressful, nonproductive, forty-five-minute commute each way for a job they hate? Who wants to sit in an office and listen to people they don't like? Who wants to do unnecessary stuff they feel is meaningless? Who wants to miss their kid's ballet recital?

No one. Not anymore.

It is life-giving to offer someone meaning in their job and also have the flexibility to live their lives. I've seen it. At my company, I offer it. I watch employees from corporate America come into our business, and it's as if they don't believe what I am offering them is possible. They think this company and their job is not real! They literally have to go through a period of detox when they join our business. It takes a while to wash the corporate off of them.

People on all levels of the organizational chart want to live in this virtual workplace reality. It's not just the front-of-the-line employees. Contractors want it. Management wants it. Executives want it. Owners want it.

EVEN GRANDMAS ARE AT THE LEDGE

I often talk to potential clients who tell me they don't know if they could get used to talking to their assistants if they are not present in the office. My response is always this, "Okay, so you can get behind the idea that you can send emails and texts. You can get behind the idea that when you get on a phone call, your phone converts your voice into an electrical signal that is then transmitted as a radio wave and then back into sound and into the ear of someone somewhere on the planet (maybe thousands of miles away). But you can't get behind the idea that maybe you can communicate with your assistant who is at home forty-seven miles down the road?"

Taking the leap isn't as farfetched as you would imagine: we're already living on the edge of the technology cliff. You use technology every day of your life. Ninety-year-old grandmas who stood in soup lines through The Great Depression are able to FaceTime with their grandchildren! If they can do it, you can, too. The leap isn't as far as people may think.

In this book, I will outline the benefits for a business of

moving to a virtual organization and employing remote workers. I'm going to prove to you that this is a viable concept and something you can implement at your company.

Once I convince you of the merits, then I'm going to teach you how to create or shift to a virtual organization. You'll learn where to start and what to prioritize.

Some of the topics I will cover might seem obvious, but I want to make sure that everyone is on the same page and that my methods are clear. My methods have worked for me. They are suggestions for you. In building your own virtual culture, you'll need to make it uniquely yours because employees and contractors value authenticity.

I'm going to show you how the world is already full of virtual workers who are working right under your nose without you even realizing it. More people work virtually than people know. There are many cases (and more and more cases every day) where companies are utilizing virtual employees in unique and unheard-of ways. For instance, some fast-food restaurants in California have hired remote workers in Nebraska to answer the speaker boxes at drive-thrus. You would never know that someone more than one thousand miles away was taking your burger order! We'll explore some other case studies further in the book.

There are countless ways to leverage technology today in a virtual environment, and I want people to understand the revolution that is happening right in front of their eyes.

This book will not delve into the argument for or against calling your employees "contractors" or "employees." We will not talk about the merits or issues with W-2s compared to 1099s. We'll leave that discussion (I mean, painfully boring debate) in the capable hands of the IRS and the Department of Labor.

While BELAY is an all-virtual company, I prefer my corporate team be here in metro Atlanta. The reason I did this in the beginning was that I couldn't afford to put everyone on a plane to hang out with us at our quarterly company meetings. I also require my contractors to be living in the United States It is important to me and my wife to keep our money in the US economy. This is a rule that I have set for our company; however, it is not necessary for everyone when converting to a virtual workforce. I will explore this topic a little later on.

TIPPING OVER THE WATERCOOLER

The watercooler in a traditional corporate office environment is the absolute worst place. It has become the symbol of a place that ends productivity, and it is a place where gossip begins. It's the place in an office that sucks the soul right out of the employee. As a hardworking person, it represents everything that I am against in Corporate America.

However, the watercooler isn't the real problem. It's the leader. When I see a leader whose employees are gossipy, unproductive, and just time-clock punching I want to grab him by his collar and shake him. I want to shout at him, "Your employees are sick and tired and done with this environment. They don't want to sit in that cubicle. They don't want to spend almost 11 days per year in their car to work here. They want a place of meaning and they need YOU to step up and create a better workplace environment! A workplace environment that is flexible, meaningful, and treats them like an adult!"

You feel me yet?

This is my Manifesto.

It's time to change. The world is demanding it. Will you heed the warning and take up the call?

I'm here to invade the workplace, topple the watercooler, liberate employees, and help you create a virtual workforce with a killer culture that produces epic results.

CHAPTER 1

LET'S BURY HENRY FORD

—

TIMES THEY ARE A-CHANGIN'

INDUSTRIAL AGE ORGANIZATION NEED NOT APPLY

The workforce is changing, and the workplace must change along with it.

We must bury Henry Ford. Don't get me wrong, I like Henry Ford. He helped to grow our nation. His influence is still prominent in this day and age—even seventy years after his death. No, I'm not talking about the fact that Fords are still on the road today. I'm talking about his theory of scientific management and how most businesses are still run and organized based on those principles that he founded.

Henry Ford's scientific management theory, in short, required that all of his employees come in to the manufacturing plant, line up next to each other, and work hard while managers circled around them like hawks. The managers were there to make sure they squeaked out every ounce of productivity.

The setup made sense for Ford. He had conveyor belts that required lines of people to physically be there to piece together each part in the straightest path to efficiency.

Although most companies don't have conveyor belts anymore, they still operate like they do and treat their employees like they do. If you think about what offices look like today, it's the same thing, just in a slightly different flavor. They put people in lines of cubicles and put managers around them to make sure they are doing what they need to do.

This organizational model, however, is a holdout from the industrial age and has no place in our evolving workplace.

That's why we should bury Henry Ford. He was a pioneer and designed a massively beautiful and ingenious system... for his day. But that was then. This is now. We need to continue to evolve.

The workforce has changed a lot since the Industrial Revolution. First, technology has made it so people don't have to do the actual work anymore. For the most part, people no longer create products with their hands; they man the machines that create the products.

Second, the consolidation of computing power changed how work was done when it evolved from a massive machine that took over five rooms to something that can be held in the palm of your hand. Work is no longer a tangible thing that you do with your hands; rather, it is an executable service that only requires the brain.

No longer do employees need to stand in a line along a conveyor belt assembling the parts of a sewing machine. They can execute their work from an airplane, a coffee shop—heck—even on the back of a galloping horse if they wanted to.

So, what's the problem in all of this? To me, it's obvious: Why does anyone go to an office? People are beginning to ask that very question. Many of them are saying "no more" to it. They're giving their employers the one-finger salute.

WHY MAKE YOUR EMPLOYEES MISERABLE?

Coupled with this tension is this: employee satisfaction and engagement is at an all-time low.

In the book *The Founder's Mentality*, Chris Zook and James Allen highlight that "a recent Gallup survey shows that only 13 percent of employees say that they are emotionally engaged with their company."

That saddens me; it's pathetic. I would like to think people deserve to work a job that has meaning to them. They want to feel connected—not only with their heads, but with their hearts as well.

TECHNOLOGY GETS A ROUND OF APPLAUSE

The necessary tooling for a virtual workforce is cheap and easy to get. All virtual employees need is a computer, a Wi-Fi connection, a webcam or telephone, and a quiet space to work. At BELAY, we provide our employees with a litany of web-based applications to help them stay connected and manage their workload. We use applications like Basecamp, Infusionsoft, Dropbox, and Zoom to get the work done. We will explore more tooling tips later on.

YOU CAN ESCAPE!

You can choose not to do business in the old industrial-age paradigm. Instead, you can move to a new paradigm that I call "virtual culture." If you move to this new paradigm, you will see greater results. You will achieve more. You will generate a healthier bottom line. You will be able to grow and scale better. You will see your influence spread. Lastly, you will be able to connect your employees' hearts to your business because, by giving them the opportunity to work how they want to work, they will produce more for your organization.

If you don't see this now, you will see it soon. You will watch big businesses crumble under the weight of this transformation if they don't ride its wave. It's a workplace apocalypse.

THE NEW PARADIGM WILL LOOK LIKE...

What will this new paradigm look like? I have a clear vision for a template.

ORGANIZATION WILL CHANGE

As we discussed before, organization models were designed to control the worker. Marissa Mayer required her employees to be present because she didn't trust her employees to get their work done.

Now, however, productivity doesn't mean that you have to sit in your seat. Using your computer and phone, you can be productive from anywhere.

ARCHITECTURE WILL BE REIMAGINED

Rows of cubicles and corner offices won't be necessary; in fact, they'll all go away. Many people will be free to work from wherever they please because their jobs don't have to be done onsite. Space needs of corporations will change to create a more agile, flexible, and fluid work environment.

LEADERSHIP ROLES WILL EVOLVE

Leadership and managers will no longer be tasked with supervising work because they believe it won't get done without their observation. Visibility (I can't see you, I can't control you) is a depreciating currency. Now, instead of seeing results from face-to-face interaction, we will see results connected to treating people like adults. Coworkers will move to a more trusting relationship.

Part of why employee satisfaction is low is because employees don't feel trusted. If an employee felt more trusted, she or he would feel more connected to the mission and the business. When employees care, they want to work harder for their leader.

We have spent a lot of time thinking about how to make this new type of leader-employee relationship come to life. We wanted our employees to understand that our default mode is trust. So, I looked around for inspiration.

I found it in my pastor. He has what he calls the "Rules of Engagement," which is a list of how he is to treat his employees and how his employees are to treat each other. I loved it so much that I stole it from him. I stole every last bit of it...sorry Andy!

In the rules of engagement, we explicitly tell our employees that when something goes wrong, our default (and their default mode as an employee) is to trust. We want our employees to address the issue and say, "Listen, we have a gap. You said X, and you didn't do it." They must assume trust. They must assume that the person who screwed up didn't do so purposefully. Lastly, if you go to your coworker and cannot resolve the issue and the gap still exists, you must take the problem up...not sideways and definitely not down.

There is a lack of trust among employees in corporate America. Their default is suspicion.

When there is trust, you will see a healthier bottom line. I see how happy my employees are to work here, and I see how it translates directly to our success. I don't ignore that symptom; I am very much coin-operated. I like making money. I like when my bottom line is healthy.

WHAT DOES WORKING VIRTUALLY LOOK LIKE?

When people think "working virtually," they mostly think of people who work from home. However, it is more than that. Virtual workers can work everywhere. They might prefer to work at a coffee shop, work outside, or work in the waiting room at their doctor's office. In essence, virtual workers can get the job done from anywhere.

My team can work from wherever they want as long as they have a quiet space, a solid laptop, a robust webcam, and a fast Wi-Fi connection.

WHAT ROLES ARE TYPICALLY FILLED BY VIRTUAL EMPLOYEES?

People forget that the traditional salesperson in many industries has been working remotely for decades. They had to be! Sometimes, those salespeople had to work in a region that was far from their headquarters and so they worked from the road and hotel rooms.

Many people think immediately of a virtual executive assistant or secretary. They aren't wrong; virtual assistants are in hot demand. By 2018, the global virtual assistant industry will exceed five billion dollars.[1]

---

1   Virtual Assistant Trends in 2016. (n.d.). Retrieved December 13, 2017, from http://ennovationconsulting.net/virtual-assistant-trends-2016/

Although those roles are a major part of the industry, there are countless other roles that are filled by virtual employees. The number and variety of those roles is growing each day.

- Virtual accountants and bookkeepers will be a $160 billion by 2018.[2]
- Virtual Webmasters is currently a $20 billion industry with a 7.1 percent annual growth rate.[3]

These numbers are not projections for some time in the distant future. They are projections for next year and two years from now. The revolution is happening now. This is very real.

We aren't talking about hypothetical roles in hypothetical industries. We are talking about well-established jobs that have been around in the traditional workplace environment. We are talking about the same role, but that role is now taking place outside the four walls of an office. We are talking about how those roles can be reevaluated and enhanced by going virtual.

2   A. (2017, July 21). Bookkeeping Buzz: Hiring a Virtual Bookkeeping Company: The Time Is Now. Retrieved December 13, 2017, from http://www.thejeffersonchronicle. com/bookkeeping-buzz-hiring-virtual-bookkeeping-company-time-now/

3   Internet Hosting Services in the US: Market Research Report. (n.d.). Retrieved December 13, 2017, from https://www.ibisworld.com/industry-trends/specialized-market-research-reports/technology/computer-services/internet-hosting-services. html

For instance, consider some of these cool applications of virtual workers.

MEDICAL PERSONNEL IN RURAL HOSPITALS

Often, remote hospitals don't have access to doctors who specialize in certain fields. What happens when a patient comes in who needs to see a specialist? Well, some doctors are now working virtually. So, all that needs to happen is for one of the nurses to strap an iPad onto a robot, turn on the webcam, and boom! That patient is now sitting in front of the specialist he needs to see. No travel, no wait times. The patient gets the help he needs when he needs it.

VIRTUAL RECEPTIONISTS WORKING FROM ACROSS THE COUNTRY

There is a company in Vegas that employs live receptionists who remotely greet people when they walk into the foyer of an office. These receptionists are sitting at home in Maryland while talking to a customer in Los Angeles!

COURT REPORTERS

The court reporting industry has been turned upside down. Instead of employing a court reporter, they place a microphone in the courtroom, record the session, and that recording is sent overnight to a company in Nepal that employs hundreds of people who each receive a seven-second snippet of the court session recording. Each person listens to their seven-second snippet, types the words they hear, and then they snip together those hundreds of people's typed pieces. The whole session is fully transcribed almost instantaneously. They even have a super cheap way to ensure quality control: They chop up the audio and give each person a different seven-second snippet to transcribe. They stitch the full transcription together, compare it to the first, fix issues, and boom! It's sent back within minutes.

HOW DO YOU KNOW IF YOUR COMPANY IS VIRTUAL READY?

We have stereotypes for everything. Most are hurtful, but some are useful. Sometimes they help us to see ourselves clearly.

I believe that in the work environment, these sorts of stereotypes might help leaders understand their businesses better.

In fact, I have a few statements I'd like you to review and analyze so that maybe you can see your business more clearly. If you identify with even one of these statements, your organization may be a workplace dinosaur or certainly trending in that direction.

Your organization might be a workplace dinosaur if...

- You aren't on social media.
- You still think you have to do everything within the business because you "are the best at it and can't find any good people."
- You have a designated parking spot at the front of your office with a sign that proudly reads "Reserved Parking for CEO."
- You aren't looking ahead a year or two down the line because you think casting vision is unnecessary. Worse yet, you use an org chart to cast vision.
- You expect great responsiveness from your employees but as their leader you are 200+ unread emails deep in your inbox.
- Your employees keep coming to you with company problems and no suggested ways to solve the problem.
- You have video cameras installed over your employee's cubicles.
- You hold a weekly company meeting that really only benefits one person's ego.
- You're finding that you can't attract and keep leaders because you mandate that they come into the office.
- You put your head in the sand when your employees

ask for workplace flexibility. Under your breath you call them "Millennials."

- At the annual Christmas party, you stand in the corner and make your employees come to you.
- Your employees can't tell you what the company mission, vision, and values are. You ask and they are like deer in headlights.
- When your employee asks if they can work from home one day per week, you assume they are lazy.
- You hear your employees communicate in the third-person way too much when a problem arises.
- You think that your company culture will be better because you approved "Business Casual Fridays."

I could go on and on and on. I see and hear this stuff all the time. Some of it is funny. Some of it is sad. Most of it is ridiculous. I speak with leaders who are either stuck or desperate for a workplace environment change and the symptoms are right there in front of their face. And, here is one of my biggest...

You are still paying rent/lease for an office no one wants to come to. As you likely know, rent is a massive expense for any business, but guess what? You don't have to be a slave to your rent any longer. By evolving your workplace into a virtual one, you can slash rent and other key costs in tangible and intangible ways. Ways that you never thought were possible.

CHAPTER 2

BENJAMINS AND INTANGIBLE BLING

———

When companies move out of a physical office and into a virtual work environment, two things are going to happen: both the employer and the employee are going to see lower costs (Benjamins!) and intangible rewards (Bling!). It's a win-win!

BENJAMINS: FINANCIAL SAVINGS BECAUSE OF REDUCED COSTS

Three and a half years ago, I felt like my company had grown to the point where I needed an office. I know, I know, it sounds completely crazy now, but hear me out. I thought that getting an office was just what you did when you were on your way up; I felt like it was a rite of passage. So, I started conducting research on what I would need in my new office and how much it would all cost.

I did not like what I discovered.

I learned that you are required to assign each employee a certain amount of square feet. That was cool with me. I was looking at giving my employees one hundred square feet each, which loosely translates into a ten-foot-by-ten-foot space. Some would say that is generous while others wouldn't, but I felt that it was fair. Then, I had to consider grossing factors like wall thickness, cubicle width, hallways, bathrooms, break rooms, windows, stairwells and other stuff you'd obviously come to expect to see in a twenty-first-century office such as Ping-Pong tables, beer kegs, and bouncy houses.

Once I tallied all of those costs, the total was cool with me. What was not cool with me, however, was by the time I added up all the space that I would need, I was looking at a facility that would have cost me about $100,000 a year, or around $8,300 a month!

Uncool.

That didn't include the build-out, which would have put me in at another one hundred thousand dollars right out of the gate. Then I would have to consider permits, licenses, maintenance, security, utilities, and insurance. It sounded like a lot, but this is a relatively cheap price tag to put thirty-some-odd people in an office.

Very uncool.

But still, I couldn't shake those numbers.

"One hundred thousand dollars a year for a lease. Eighty-three hundred dollars a month toward rent. A three-thousand-dollar security deposit. All that money down the drain."

I couldn't stop thinking about all the other great things I could do with that money. I could ramp up my employees' already kick-ass benefits! I could expand my team! (I kept hearing that voice in the back of my head whispering to me, "If you stop growing, you die.") I could network! I could invest it back into the company! I could afford to give maternity and paternity leave! I could give my employees paid volunteer time off! We could grow, grow, grow.

After talking with my wife and praying on it, I finally came to the conclusion that I was being crazy, I was going with the crowd, and I was doing what everyone else does. I wasn't being different. I wasn't holding true to the meaning of the company. If I had moved us to an office, I would have been a hypocrite. We were selling virtual services to other companies, but we couldn't stay virtual ourselves? I couldn't imagine how those sales calls would have gone.

I opted out of moving into an office. Truth be told, I'm so glad that I did. Instead of losing all of that money to an office, I was able to offer my employees all of the incredible benefits that I wanted to.

I felt that pressure of moving into an office, but I decided to take a different path and keep my team virtual. I made the right choice because the lion's share of my employees (easily over 90 percent of them) said, "Thank you for not making us move to an office! I want to work from home. That's why I came here to work for you to begin with!" The office would have changed everything that my employees had come to love about their virtual lives. It would have added that expensive and time-consuming commute back to their daily schedule. It would have destroyed their flexible days. It would have cost them more money to do less work.

There are other leaders out there who are probably struggling with this very decision right now: Do I get an office and take a hit on that massive expense? They are probably mulling over the same things that I did. They probably think moving to an office is just the next logical step in the life cycle of their business, just like going to college, getting a job, and getting married is a part of the human life cycle. It's just something that you do.

But they don't have to. There are other options.

Run the numbers; you'll see just how enormous the cost savings is by not moving to an office. Keep in mind, going virtual does not just save you from paying rent. It also saves you money on all the other crap you suddenly don't have to buy. No trash cans, no whiteboards, no drinks to stock your fridge.

Have your CFO run your numbers to see just how extraordinary the cost savings are. You can use our Office Space Calculator at http://virtualculturebook.com/officespace to calculate your potential office costs!

LIFEWAY RAN THE NUMBERS

One of BELAY's customers, and now a dear personal friend, is Dr. Thom Rainer, the CEO of LifeWay, a 5,600-employee-large, multi-million-dollar organization. It is an older organization; therefore, it is appropriately traditional. But a couple of years ago, Dr. Rainer began a brave, new initiative to send 75 percent of his employees back home to work.

Why did he do this? Easy. Chief among many other reasons (which I will talk about later on), he was sick of his real estate. His offices were expensive to maintain, and the costs grew as his buildings aged. It made a lot of sense; think about all of those heating, cooling, lighting, and cleaning costs wasted on meeting rooms that are only used 2 percent of the time.

Dr. Rainer has already sold about 75 percent of their 1.1 million square feet of corporate real estate in downtown Nashville. They are consolidating the 25 percent of their workforce left into a new, smaller 250,000-square-foot facility in downtown Nashville.

It's one of the bravest corporate initiatives I've ever witnessed. I'm so proud that BELAY is a part of it.

LifeWay hired us to provide them with virtual assistants. By going virtual, not only is LifeWay saving money on office space, but they are also saving on employment burden cost (more on this later). Virtual assistants are more productive; therefore, they can work fewer hours and cost less money than traditional assistants. LifeWay also doesn't have to give them benefits because they are not a traditional employee.

My company also solves another problem for Life-Way: the fact that secretarial and administrative jobs are inherently unattractive to employees. Great talent does not come out of college and say, "I really would love to become an assistant." Many people see only a dead-end for administrative jobs. They don't aspire to be an assistant.

My company solves that problem because we have talented people who are qualified but who don't or can't work a full-time, in-office job. You don't need to hire them; all you have to do is pay a subscription fee to us. It's a win-win. Talented people producing great results.

LIFEWAY IS A LARGE ORGANIZATION, BUT SMALL COMPANIES CAN ALSO SEE SAVINGS

There is a reason why there are no less than twenty-seven million "small businesses" in the United States with less than one million dollars in sales. They don't understand where their money is going. They have employees with a seventeen-dollar-an-hour wage and an annual salary of thirty-five thousand dollars. But when you add up all of the employment burden costs, the adjusted hourly wage is truly $30.87. That is a cost increase of 82 percent! That employee who you think you are spending thirty-five thousand dollars per year on actually costs fifty-five thousand dollars! That is a huge hit for small businesses and can make a real dent in growth and revenue.

Small businesses often stay small because of things like this.

Something that could help them grow is understanding where those costs are and how to cut them by moving some of their employees to virtual.

The cost savings impact of moving to a virtual workforce would be even greater for those small businesses. Eliminating a huge expense like a lease would allow those companies access to more capital to grow their business. I will repeat myself here: if you stop growing, you die. No business remains static; you are either in growth or in decline.

I have a friend who owns a small business. He got an office because he thought that was what he should do. He watched my business grow while his faltered. He asked me what the deal was.

"It's because I have no major costs other than payroll," I said. "I don't throw away money on a lease."

He asked himself, "Do I really need an office?" The answer: no.

I suggested that he disband his office and allow his employees to work from home. It was an easy fix, he saved a ton of money, and his employees are markedly happier. During those quarterly meetings when they absolutely need to get together, they rent a room at a place like WeWork, Roam, or Blueprint +Co. or sit in a restaurant or a library.

BLING, AKA INTANGIBLE BENEFITS

Bling is that intangible reward that virtual companies can enjoy because of their virtual nature.

THE SOUL-SUCKING COMMUTE

One of my favorite examples of bling is the ten hours a week that virtual employees get back because they don't have to commute to an office. In Atlanta, the average commute time is forty-two minutes each way. If you have a job where you have two weeks off for vacation, you are looking at spending an equivalent of 15.6 days sitting in your car per year. On the flip side, if you go virtual, you gain a half of a month of your life back each year. If your commute is sixty minutes per way, you are losing 20.8 days per year. If you are one of the 3.6 million people in America whose commute is a whopping ninety minutes each way, your commute is 31.3 days per year. That is one twelfth of your year wasted in your car! God help these people!

Consider this excerpt taken from an article published in the Washington Post...

According to the [US] Census, there were a little over 139 million workers commuting in 2014. At an average of twenty-six minutes each way to work, five days a week, fifty weeks a year, that works out to something like a total of 1.8 trillion minutes Americans spent commuting in 2014. Or, if you prefer, call it 29.6 billion hours, 1.2 billion days, or a collective 3.4 million years. With that amount of time, we could have built nearly three hundred Wikipedias, or built the Great Pyramid of Giza *twenty-six times*—all in 2014 alone.

Could you imagine a world where you could fully eliminate that commute? Think of the productivity! Think of the quality of life that people would suddenly be able to access!

Let's consider those poor souls who commute ninety minutes each way, each day. If they were suddenly allowed to work virtually, they could potentially give back their employer three hours of productivity a day, or 750 extra hours per year. Do you hear me owners, leaders, hiring managers, and employers? 750 extra hours. 750 hours in one, single year!

According to the article, if you lowered those ninety-minute commutes to thirty minutes per way, you would create an extra "1.8 billion man-hours of potential productivity" that could be "released back into the economy. That's the time equivalent of nine hundred thousand full-time jobs."

THE NO-FEAR FLEXIBILITY

Another intangible benefit that falls under the bling category is the workplace flexibility that comes with going virtual. If you are a virtual employee and you need to take your kid to the doctor at 10:00 a.m. on a Tuesday, do it. You can tend to your sick child without guilt because you aren't punching a clock.

Lisa (lovingly nicknamed LZ) is my CFO, and she is also a mom. LZ came to us from a traditional corporate environment and so is still not fully used to the flexibility that her virtual job affords her. I like to call what she is going through "corporate detox." It's a common phenomenon... almost every employee who comes to me from the corporate world deals with it.

One day, I was on the phone with LZ, and I could hear some kids talking in the background. I asked her what was going on, and she said, "Sorry, I'm with my kid, I'm standing here with her at the bus stop."

I said, "What?! Why are you on the phone with me? Go enjoy your time with your kid."

She told me, "No, I can do the call."

But I wouldn't let her. The whole point of our company and our mission is to allow LZ and everyone else the time they need to live their lives and still produce a quality business result.

I made her hang up the phone.

Later, she told me that conversation impacted her. Because she had been in a traditional work environment for so long, she hadn't realized just how far she had pushed away her personal life for her work life. She didn't grasp how much she had sacrificed. She told me that moment made her understand what my company offered her, and that was so meaningful to her.

It is meaningful to me, too. I hope we can impact the futures of kids whose moms and dads can suddenly invest more hours in the day in them. To me, that is a big deal. It is an intangible gift that is priceless.

In our virtual company, you can be flexible without fear. In other companies that are not virtual, that just isn't true.

In many cases, you can't be flexible at all. In others, you can be flexible, but you're going to pay for it. They're going to dock you for taking time off to take your kid to a 10:00 a.m. doctor's appointment and not being present in the office. That's just the way Corporate America behaves and it's stupid. You and I both know that.

ENVIRONMENTAL STEWARDSHIP

There is also the intangible reward of environmental stewardship. Being virtual is green. When you work virtually, you use less paper. You don't have an office space, which requires a lot of energy for conditioned environment and electricity. You use less gas in your car, and you contribute less to pollution because you are no longer commuting. Companies with virtual workers can tell a great story about their clean impact on the environment.

Personally, I believe in God. I also believe that He created the Earth. I believe that He gave me a season of time on the Earth to be a good steward of it and within it. For me, this is not a red or blue issue, this not a Republican or Democrat issue. Taking care of the Earth is a stewardship issue; stewarding what has been entrusted to us. By creating a virtual workplace you are actually helping the environment...period.

In the past, the overwhelming belief about working virtually was that it was an illegitimate way to produce work. People believed that the only way "real work" happened was in an office. The truth is, we are far more productive outside of an office than in it.[1]

Although the underlying belief has been proven false, the dogma of virtual hate still exists. Workers now want to work from home, and those who do are the objects of envy. Yet some still snub them.

There is a tension in the American workforce between the desire to work from home and the negative stigma associated with it. I see this tension, but I think it will go away over time as the stigma disappears. The more you lean virtual, the less stigma is involved with it, and the more virtual workers can come out of the shadows.

THE COMPANY GETS BLING TOO

Bling is also awarded to the company when it moves to virtual. One of the greatest gifts leaders within the company receive from moving to virtual is a more productive

---

1   Evans, J. (2017, August 13). Not even remotely possible. Retrieved December 13, 2017, from https://techcrunch.com/2017/08/13/not-even-remotely-possible/?utm_ source=pocket&utm_medium=email&utm_campaign=pockethits

workforce. That is because virtual work lends itself to result-based work.

What do I mean by result-based work? It is pretty simple... employers send virtual employees work. The virtual employees complete the work. Then the work gets sent back. End of story. In a virtual world, employees who are just there to punch a clock are found out fast. Those who are only focused on getting paid and wasting time will find themselves out of the company quickly.

In the virtual world, employers can figure out the bad apples from the good quickly. They can fix hiring mistakes faster than they would otherwise.

That's a huge win for an employer and a company when you push in the virtual direction. It forces the nature of the people working for you to become more results-oriented.

THERE ARE OTHER INTANGIBLE REWARDS AS WELL...

One of the greatest benefits of hiring virtually is that owners can hire people who live where the local pay scale is less than where the company is located.

For my clients, this is a huge deal.

A client of ours, a CFO inside of a well-known Bay Area tech company, was in the market for a new assistant. The problem was, he was living and working out of the Silicon Valley paradigm. The same place that is enamored by unicorns. Why is that a problem? Well, a highly qualified executive assistant out there in the Bay Area would cost around one hundred thousand dollars a year plus benefits, bonus, and a significant employment burden cost. He specifically requested that I connect him with a virtual assistant who lived where the pay scale was less—preferably somebody who was hardworking and had good values for way less cost.

He asked me if this was a pipe dream.

I told him, "No, that isn't a pipe dream. I can get you that exact person. They're everywhere."

He was dumbfounded. He didn't believe that I could do it. I told him that he had been in Silicon Valley for too long drinking that overpriced Bay Area Kool-Aid. I assured him that there were great workers in the US who demanded less.

We found him a qualified virtual assistant out of the Midwest for a quarter of the cost. She worked out great, and he is a believer now.

Not only did we save him seventy-five thousand dollars, but we also saved him from having to pay all of the incidentals required for a full-time employee because his assistant was virtual and therefore no longer had to work full time. This is not atypical; we usually find that when we take on a new client like this one, we can replace people who work on-site for thirty to thirty-five hours per week with a virtual employee who only needs to work about fifteen to twenty hours per week. When we first started the business, I could not predict that reduction, but after many years, I can factually back up this business claim of ours.

It's not that those virtual employees are doing less. They are just not distracted, so they can do more in a shorter amount of time. They don't have to do all of the corporate stuff, such as unnecessary meetings. They're focused people who get stuff done. They're college-educated, stay-at-home moms and dads who have past business and professional experience and who could jump in and start helping you right away. They're results-oriented because they want to get the job done and go back to their life on a day-to-day basis. That is just like my whole corporate team here in Atlanta. We get so much done because we are all results-oriented rather than task-oriented. We don't just give our employees a list of tasks; we tell them what results are expected of them. Results trump tasks at BELAY.

When we found that assistant for our client, the cost savings blew his mind. That amount of cost savings was not a one-off; that percentage is pretty standard for my company to deliver.

Early on in the business, I was talking to a guy at an organization in Dallas who wanted to use BELAY. He said that he only had the budget to hire one full-time executive assistant in Dallas. He was budgeting around sixty thousand dollars for one. I asked him if he considered the employment burden cost of hiring someone. He hadn't. So, I told him that, usually, it is about 50 percent of the employee salary (it might even be higher with bigger companies because benefits are typically richer). So, he was looking at ninety thousand dollars to hire and employ an assistant.

I told him that I could find five virtual assistants at ten hours per week for him and the rest of his leadership all for sixty thousand dollars. No employment burden cost. He couldn't have been more thrilled, and we got him set up right away. They're so elated with the service that they've added many more assistants and are still happy clients today.

Of course, I could take it a step further and find him someone in the Philippines (or some other developing country) for two thousand dollars a year. But there is a steep diminishing cost that is tangible and intangible. Barriers like language, time zone, culture, and even religion plague the lesser-cost services found in developing countries. Even though the employment price tag drops, the quality of the service or the barriers experienced connected to the person drop so much that it is just not worth it from what our clients tell us. The trade-off becomes detrimental. Plus, although they are remote, they are often still housed in an office among a bay of cubicles, which contradicts our whole mission.

We are just so different from overseas virtual services. We are the Tesla; they are the Saturn.

That's the intangible in all of this: you get a greater result at less cost, which means more margin, and as owners of our business, that's the big bottom line.

BEING VIRTUAL ALLOWED BELAY TO HIRE IN THE US

I am proud of the fact that we have found a way to keep hiring costs down while still hiring in the US. I'm even more proud that we've shared that ability with our clients.

I just love America. The country has got problems, but I

love this place. I'm proud to live here, and I thank God daily for being born in the US.

I have patriotism. I owe something to this country, and I feel a sense of responsibility for its well-being. So, I made a conscious decision to hire in the US. I wanted to impact the US economy, and I took this mission to heart after the collapse of 2008. At that time, I looked around and saw so many people right here in my own backyard suffering because they needed jobs.

The US national unemployment rate was 9.6 percent in 2010. Everyone was out of work, including many professional, white-collar people. So, résumés were flying at BELAY, and I had the labor supply. On the other hand, companies couldn't afford to hire but still needed administrative and bookkeeping services. They needed to find a way around the costs. They had zero desire to increase headcount. BELAY was there to fill that need.

We still average over 1,100 résumés a month, so we the opportunity to pick from the very best of the best.

NEXT STEPS

Convinced yet? I understand it is easy for me to say to you that I can save you $X amount of money in wages. But

I want you to realize wage is only a factor of how much your employees realistically cost you. What about all of the countless other variables that go into determining cost? What about those variables such as benefits, office supplies, hardware—heck—even the cost to provide AC for an employee or clean drinking water? There are so many factors, and as my team and I talked to more and more business owners and leaders, we realized that many of them have never taken those costs into account.

Our sales team encounters this all of the time. They will talk to business owners and ask them what the business owner's desired per hour rate is. Let's say that the owner says it is thirty-seven bucks an hour for an executive assistant. The problem is that that owner (like my friends in Dallas) is only thinking about wage; he isn't thinking about all of the other costs.

At BELAY, we created an employment burden calculator to show leaders and owners what they were spending on their employees. I urge you to check out our employment burden calculator to determine your real costs. We provide the resource for free on our website at http://virtualculturebook.com/employeeburden.

CHAPTER 3

NO MORE PLAYPENS FOR ADULTS

———

THE MODERN ADULT PLAYPEN

How are your employees arranged? That is the first thing an executive or business owner interested in creating a virtual organization should ask himself. Are they arranged in cubicles? In rows? At big, open tables? In their own separate offices?

I am willing to bet that cubicles populate your office layout. I don't mean to be nasty; an overwhelming majority of modern offices are cubicle farms.

That is just the reality of our time.

Once you picture how your employees are arranged, ask yourself, "Why are they arranged that way?"

In the case of the business owner who has placed his employees into cubicles, he has done so because he wants complete control. That leader does not care how much his employees hate their cubicles. He does not care that they reek of an antiquated management style from Ford's era. The leader continues to keep his employees in cubicles because those cubicles are meant to act as control mechanisms for employees; they are adult playpens.

Cubicles allow managers to keep a close eye on their employees because they keep employees rounded up in one central area that is easy to oversee. This feature is particularly important to some leaders who believe, "If I can't see my employees, I can't control them." They fear this might lead to lower productivity if leaders were to give up centralized office space.

Some people will read this and think, "That isn't me. I'm not afraid, I just really need to have an office space. I like it when my team meets to collaborate or solve complex problems."

I've heard that excuse a hundred different times in a hundred different ways, but it is crap. You can do all those things virtually. But people use them as an excuse because they don't want to admit why they really don't want to go virtual: their fear of losing control.

Fear is connected to control, but it goes deeper than that. The fear primarily stems from trust. "Can I trust my employees?" If you can trust them, that need for control goes away. That fear evaporates.

But most people lack trust. There is a saying: hurt people hurt people. I think it's true. People who are not hurt typically don't approach situations under the assumption that other people have the intention to hurt them. They trust them. On the other hand, folks who have been hurt approach situations fearful that they will be hurt again. That fear results in negative crap that ends up hurting other people. The chain continues.

I understand it is daunting to give up the complete control that cubicles allow when considering going virtual. But I could argue that there is a better way that's more productive and will produce a greater result: let your employees work where they want. It will impact your bottom line in a positive way.

I know that may feel impossible. It takes a big leap of faith to evolve from a control-and-fear-based environment to a trust-based environment where you don't feel as if you must have a close eye on your employees.

Some people will say that the chasm between fear/control and trust seems too wide to cross. They will say it will take too long or be too costly and then reason it away. But I know that there is a group of people out there that are brave. They're going to jump the chasm and see how drastically it changes their workforce. It's powerful.

All you have to do is say to your employees, "I trust you to do the right thing."

Uttering this phrase will help you jump the chasm. Once you, the leader, crosses, everyone on your team will follow.

My company is proof that it works. As a leader, I do my very best to approach every situation with trust. I trust that my employees are adults who are going to do what they say. I trust my employees to get their work done even when I don't see them. I trust that they care about being at work. I trust that they want to do the best job they can. I trust that sometimes expectations will not be met, but that is okay. I trust that my employees want to meet those expectations and that they will get there. I trust that my employees want to make this an awesome company and that they believe in what we're doing.

Not only have I told my six-hundred-plus team members that I trust them in some way, but I have taught them to trust each other. Because I operate under the assumption of trust rather than fear, my employees do the same. That trust trickles down throughout the whole organization. They have carried on this cornerstone idea of trust and have woven it into our culture. This trust is the bedrock of our successful virtual workforce. I like to call it trickle-down trust.

When I start a relationship with a new employee, I have a conversation with them about three things. First, I tell them to enjoy their new job. Second, I explain to them that I trust them to take care of their job and the company. Third, I tell them to trust that I have their best interest in mind.

It is a profoundly powerful conversation. I have found that it impacts my employees because they immediately understand the joy of having a boss who trusts and cares for them. It makes them work harder because they don't want to do anything that might impact that trust. It also makes them understand that they can come clean on mistakes or mishaps because they know that I am open to having those hard discussions. They become natural defenders of the culture. Who wouldn't want committed employees who act as the greatest guardians of something you worked hard to create?

THE ABSURD CASE OF THE MISSING EXECUTIVE

True Story. I have a good friend—we'll call him Sean—who is a senior marketing executive at a well-known bank here in metro Atlanta. We all know that banks give out vice-president positions like they're going out of style, but Sean is truly a senior-level guy. Even though Sean is a senior-level guy, he still sits in a cubicle.

One day, he was away from his cubicle talking to a coworker about a project in another part of the office on a different floor. While Sean was gone, his boss came by to talk to him, but Sean was not there. So, his boss left for a bit and then came back to check again. When he returned, Sean still wasn't there. When Sean got back to his cubicle, his boss was waiting for him. His boss was irate that he wasn't sitting in his seat. Naturally, Sean became pissed off, too. Being reprimanded as a grown man for not being in his seat seemed insane to him, especially considering the senior-level position he held in the organization.

Sean recounted the story to me a couple of months later. His ordeal was just mind-blowing; I couldn't understand that sort of work environment.

It was incredible to me how incensed Sean's boss became when he felt that little slip of control when he didn't see him in his cubicle. It is an antiquated, old-school dogma from the Industrial Age. This example plays out in businesses all over our country, every day.

The people at the top of organizations promulgate the need for control. They think, "I've put in my penance, I've done my time, now I'm at the top, and therefore I should be able to enjoy complete control."

It doesn't just happen in banks and hierarchical organizations; it is also rampant in these new tech companies. Leadership at these companies makes a big show about getting rid of cubicles and dreary office space. But their beer on tap, comfy sofas, nap pods, and music rooms provide the same service as cubicles. At the end of the day, it's the same thing with just a different skin on it; leadership wants people in the office so they can control them.

ENGAGEMENT ISN'T ONLY FOR WEDDINGS

In the book *The Founder's Mentality*, Chris Zook and James Allen cite a study that shows only 13 percent of employees feel engaged in and connected to their job. This statistic made me stop and think.

To be honest, it made me sad. I want people to be engaged in what they do. What's the point of going to work if your heart isn't in it? I get that, for a lot of people, their job is just a paycheck, but I hope people can one day say they come into work because they are passionate about it.

Some employees might feel guilty for not feeling engaged in their work. It's not their fault; they are a byproduct of the system that they are a part of. They are reduced to a unit of production...a cog. They are forced up or down the hierarchy of the company. If things go well, then they come out the other end with a corner office and power to wield over those below them.

As you can tell, I loathe org charts. In fact, we present org charts with the leader on the bottom of the page in our organization. This acts as a visual reminder to our employees that we value them, that they aren't just rungs at the bottom of the ladder. They have a part to play and we all contribute as a team. That mindset doesn't exist in a control environment.

My virtual employees feel more engaged than the average employee. How do I know this? I see signs of it everywhere. My employees talk about our culture as much as I do. My employees cannot shut up about how great BELAY is. They brag about our company while they are out playing Bingo with friends or on dates with their spouses. They want their friends and spouses to work for us because they are just so dang happy. When an employee is talking about how great your company is outside of traditional work hours, you've struck gold.

For example, I happened to bump into our manager of accounting at the beach, where she was enjoying a weekend away with a bunch of her girlfriends. When I saw her waiting for a table in a restaurant, I ran up to her and gave her a big hug and introduced myself to her friends. Her friends started telling me how much she talks about BELAY, how she loves working with us, and how lucky she is to have a job that she loves. It made me feel so great to hear that from them.

Once they were seated, I convinced the bartender to let me buy them a bottle of nice rosé and present it to them at the table. I started bragging about her in front of her friends. I went overboard, but it was important for me to do this because I wanted to show her just how much I truly appreciated her. I wanted to remind her that she and many like her are the reason why BELAY is so great. It was my pleasure to give back to her because she was talking about our business on a weekend getaway with her girlfriends when she didn't have to.

AN ATTITUDE OF GRATITUDE

I also know my employees are engaged because they not

only identify with our mission and six corporate values, but they can also share how they connect with them. For instance, one of our six values is gratitude. I chose gratitude as one of our values because I believe that if you really want to make a change with yourself, you must start by being grateful for all of the things you already have. We regularly show gratitude in our company, and my employees connect with gratitude through something that we call a "Frugal WOW." The Frugal WOW in BELAY has drastically impacted our culture for the better.

It is best to explain frugal wows through an example. If I hear Jessica, one of our employees, talking about how much she likes baseball, I will "Frugal WOW" her and mail her tickets to a baseball game. Any of my employees can do that for any other employee, and BELAY has a Frugal WOW budget that will pay for them to do that.

It's our way of showing gratitude; it is our way of telling our employees, "Thank you so much for helping me with that," or "You're doing an awesome job."

We send Frugal WOWs to our customers and contractors as well. We make sure that Frugal WOWs are not gifts that signify completing milestones; rather, we want them to be an act that comes out of a genuine feeling of gratitude. By allowing all of our employees the ability to show gratitude, we help them to identify with that core value that is integral to BELAY.

I want to outline some of my favorite Frugal WOW examples:

1. We sent a client a chrome fortune cookie paperweight when one of his books was published in China.
2. We pay attention to our clients' hobbies or interests. We sent BBQ spices to someone who loves to cook and monogrammed guitar picks to someone who loves to play guitar.
3. Some people on our team have sent or received gifts for no reason at all! (Candy bars, five-dollar gift cards, books, handwritten notes, etc.)

ENGAGED EMPLOYEES EQUAL PRODUCTIVE EMPLOYEES

When an employee is engaged, they are productive. When an employee is engaged with the company, they work to weave the company's why through the work that they create, which produces a powerful result.

HOW TO KNOW IF YOUR EMPLOYEES ARE SATISFIED AND ENGAGED

If your employees are leaving, then I can almost guarantee that they weren't satisfied or engaged.

Regardless of whether you're a Fortune 10 or a Fortune Nothing, if you are losing good people in your business, you must ask three very simple questions in the exit interviews: Why are you really leaving? What is the reason you are leaving? And what it the real reason you are leaving?

They're going to give you a trite answer because they just want to get out of there without burning any bridges. But you need to show them that you are a safe harbor, and you just need to know so you can make it better for the next person. Sometimes, the answer is about pay or other variables like that. But if the interviewer gets a sense that the employee's heart was never connected to the work, then you have to get to the bottom of why that is the case.

As a co-founder, I know that I won't be the person who can get to the bottom of why people are leaving. That is because my company is my baby and sometimes I'm blinded by my devotion to it. Because I think my baby is so beautiful, it is hard for me to gauge how others see it. For that reason, I rely on a handful of trusted advisors, such as my assistant, Paige, and my HR Manager, Krisha, to deliver the hard truth to me.

To make sure that employees aren't leaving because their hearts weren't in it, the leader needs to step up. Problems always start with the leader. If a company is losing top talent, the problem is with the leader, not with the employees. That leader hasn't done a good job to communicate, share, or connect the employees to the purpose of the business. If the leader isn't casting vision, if the leader isn't talking about the why and teaching it throughout the organization, then that passion will not trickle down.

Of course, a leader must be vigilant of those employees who will simply never be as engaged as is required. I learned this from one my very smart advisors. He calls those people "terminally unique." Terminally unique people are usually great people, but they usually don't last long because they are not as engaged in the business as they need to be.

Unfortunately, they have to be weeded out.

A terminally unique employee dances to their own tune. If I say to my employees that we are all going to walk through a hallway at noon, a terminally unique person will cartwheel through that hallway at 12:02 p.m. They do this to stand out. Creative companies (like ad agencies) can sometimes appreciate terminally unique people, but in most cases, they are not suitable employees in the long term. A leader needs people who consistently do what is asked of them and who participate in something that is bigger than themselves. For that reason, I steer clear of terminally unique people because I believe that it is tough for them to become fully engaged.

IS IT HOT IN HERE? HOW TO ASSESS THE TEMPERATURE IN THE ROOM

To figure out if employees are hot or cold or lukewarm to your why, here are three ways to measure the temperature:

1. FOCUS GROUPS

As a leader, you should create employee focus groups. If done right, the conversation that goes down in these meetings can tell you how your employees are feeling. What do I mean by "if done right"? You have to let your employees talk openly about things that they want to talk about. If you have created a trusting environment, your employees will open up big time.

2. SURVEYS

I could pull up countless reports online that will show me that employees are having major issues with collaboration, productivity, and distractions in the workplace. Companies are hearing it directly from their employees, but what are they doing with this information? How can they begin to treat these illnesses if they don't know who is reporting them?

That is why I try not to use anonymous surveys in my company. I believe that if you can't own it, then you can't say it.

Leaders should survey their employees to understand where they are going wrong. At BELAY, our default is to not use anonymous surveys for the most part. That is for two reasons. First, it is too easy for people to hide behind their words. They are able to run their mouth and be hurtful without any fear, which I can't stand. Second, if someone does blast something or someone in a survey, we can't address it efficiently because we don't know where it came from. Hurt people hurt people. When we first started, we allowed anonymous surveys, but it made me feel crappy because I couldn't do anything about the problems we were seeing. Since banning most anonymous surveys, we've found that our feedback has been more effective and action-oriented and has been more helpful for everyone.

It is important to include questions on these surveys that will prompt discussion that might be indicative of bad things in the long run. In my opinion, beyond maintaining and growing shareholder value, culture is the most important thing to maintain in the long run. For that reason, we focus on including many survey questions that would reveal issues with the culture.

We ask leading questions to determine if my employees understand the culture. One of the most tactical things I ask my employees to do is to give me the elevator pitch for BELAY. I expect that each employee should quickly be able to tell me what BELAY does and how we do it in thirty seconds. Every employee should be able to give me a straightforward, concise, and uniform pitch. If there is unreasonable variation, I know I am in trouble. If they can't give me that information, then that tells me they aren't engaged with what we are doing or our why.

3. KISS THIS FROG

I admit, even for leaders who try their hardest to stay in touch with employees, it is tough to feel the changes in temperature throughout the whole organization. There is a parable about a pot of water that contains a frog. The temperature of the water in the pot slowly increases and the frog barely notices...until the water is boiling. That's kind of like what it is within an organization. You are so deep in it that it is hard to feel that the water is getting hotter until it is too late. I feel that way about employee satisfaction, so I go to the people outside of the pot of water to tell me when the temperature is changing. You have to keep your eye on the thermometer. I haven't cornered the market yet.

Independent third parties ask employees in-depth questions that draw out negative symptoms. They ask, "Do you feel like your leaders are transparent with you?" and "Do you know where your company is headed in the next three to five years?"

When they compare answers, those answers should all be pretty uniform. If there is a lot of variation in answers to any one question, I'm at fault.

Because we are up for a lot of culture awards, we always have third parties talking to our employees. For instance, we won number one in Best Culture for Small-Sized Companies from *Entrepreneur Magazine*. We won it after their team came in and conducted an independent employee satisfaction assessment.

WHY DO EMPLOYEES WANT TO WORK VIRTUALLY?

And the winners are...

1. **No more long commutes!** More time with family, friends, and hobbies! I don't know of anyone who wouldn't say yes to that! Commuting is a nonproductive time suck. It can also be stressful because of heavy traffic or accidents. Commuting also puts a lot of wear and tear on your vehicle in the long run.

2. **More flexibility.** Working remotely can give you an opportunity to work around life events, personal needs, appointments, and kids' schedules. We hear it all of the time from our employees how incredible that flexibility feels...flexibility is priceless. To be there in the mornings to cook pancakes and see your child off to school is a gift.

3. **Productivity increases.** By the time you are in the labor force, most people have learned how and when they work best. Do you work best in crowded, noisy areas? In brightly lit spaces? Alone? In a group? Working virtually allows you to tailor your work environment to how you work best. Bespoke work environments increase productivity big time!

4. **Save money.** Virtual employees can save money in places that they never thought of before. For instance, they can save on business apparel, gas for commuting, and eating out during their lunch hour.

5. **Save time.** I've heard about another huge win from the women in the company; they save a ton of time getting dressed in the mornings! I guess this is true for guys, too, but I wouldn't know...I gave up on dressing up a long time ago! A T-shirt, comfortable jeans, and flip flops are my current business-casual attire. Suits and ties are for weddings and funerals.

WHAT HAPPENS WHEN EMPLOYEES FEEL TRUSTED?

When employees feel trusted, they seem to more naturally connect to what the mission, or the "big why," is. When they feel like their leaders trust them, they take ownership. They feel like they are being treated like an adult. There is just something so powerful that happens when all of these feelings come into play.

I just had this conversation with my nine-year-old son. We were sitting around the dinner table, and he was angry that his grandmother had cut up his steak for him.

"I'm not two!" he said to me. "I can do it myself!"

I understood how he felt and told him that it was okay that he felt angry. While his grandmother is a great person, the truth was he didn't need the help...period.

You can translate this scenario of my son at the dinner table to an adult in the workplace. They're both negative situations which result in some nasty feelings. When left unchecked, these feelings can build to become a quiet hatred towards the leaders and the whole mission.

That is exactly what happened to my virtual executive assistant, Paige, at the job she had held before she came to us. Before Paige moved to BELAY, her first real job was at a marketing consulting firm. It was a small business; one woman ran the show. Paige admitted that she was "just kind of miserable" while working there.

I asked her why.

She said, "I mostly felt like my work didn't matter." There was no real mission, no real communication, and no real trust. Plus, her boss wasn't a leader. She rarely came into the office. But the employees were happier that way: "We loved when she was gone," Paige said.

In 2011, Paige got pregnant with her first of three kids. She said that she saw pregnancy as her "way out" of her job. She felt like she was in jail. She decided she would never work again.

Only ten months later, after hearing about how great

BELAY was from a friend, that promise was dead in the water. Paige was hired on the spot. She is the only person in the history of my team to have been hired right on the spot. She's been my virtual assistant for five years, and we haven't looked back.

She wasn't looking for a job. She wasn't looking for anything, but she just couldn't stay away.

I wondered what made us different.

She said that it was the mission and the culture and the trust. It took her a long while to wrap her head around the fact that I trusted her. It was so different from her old job, and it took her a while to recover from the environment there. She said that working at her old company "changed who [she] was... In college, [she] was this fun, outgoing person," and then when she began her job, she had to strip herself of her emotions because she couldn't trust her boss. She "went from wearing [her] heart on [her] sleeve to leaving [her] heart at home." She was sitting in a cubicle all day and wasting a lot of time. She found herself punching a time clock and collecting a paycheck.

I helped coach her through that. A couple of weeks after she started with BELAY, I noticed that she was in a bad mood and asked her what was wrong. She told me she was still angry with her former employers. I told her that she needed to practice corporate forgiveness, giving grace to those that you work with in order heal wounds. I think it was an "aha" moment for her. She followed my advice, although she says that her "heart is still a little bit hardened." She said she could never imagine having what she has with us with her old boss. There was just a different level of trust at BELAY that made her feel more connected to her coworkers and the mission at large.

SNOWBALL EFFECT

There is a snowball effect when you create an atmosphere of trust. When my employees feel trusted, the feeling spills over into their relationships with our contractors and customers. My employees begin to assume the best in others, too.

Many companies treat customers like they are the problem. Banks are guilty of that. We all deal with employees who have completely forgotten that you are a customer. They make your life a living hell because they work in an environment that has become toxic, uncertain, fleeced with policies, and unfun.

Customers screw up sometimes, too, but when you approach problems with trust, it paves the way for a meaningful connection with the customer and the contractor. The win happens not just inside your company, but outside of it, too.

WHAT HAPPENS WHEN EMPLOYEES DON'T FEEL TRUSTED?

Let me tell you...it isn't good!

When employees don't feel trusted, they second-guess their work and don't use their energy to push forward. Instead, they move their energy to the sides or to the people underneath them. They start politicking. They'll conceal their true beliefs. They will only do the minimum amount of work required to get their manager's approval, which often translates into doing just enough so as not to get fired.

It reminds me of a scene in *Office Space*—one of my favorite movies—when Peter talks to the two Bobs. Peter works at Initech, and the company culture is so bad that everyone does just enough to keep their jobs. Peter admits that in any given week, he probably does about fifteen minutes of actual work!

Overall, when people don't feel trusted, it slows down the process of productivity in a big way.

For many large companies, their employees' productivity is as slow as molasses. However, leaders in large corporations can get around this by giving their employees gas in the form of trust.

All they have to do is make a statement: "Listen, we love you as an employee. Our default position is that we trust you. Every day when you come into work, we will allow you to do what you need to do to do the best job that you can for us."

Can you imagine how refreshing that would be to hear as an employee in a large organization? I couldn't even imagine that coming from anyone working in a Fortune 100 today. But I can imagine the impact that singular message would have on their people. They would be faster, more productive, empowered, perform better, and feel more connected to the why.

Employees are also more likely to gossip when they don't feel trusted and when leaders don't create a clear enough vision for the business. They will wonder, "What am I even doing here?"

A lack of trust creates a negative environment, and negative environments breed gossip. Gossip can come in many forms, but specifically in this scenario, gossip means taking a problem to somebody who you know can do nothing about it. For instance, turning to your coworker about an issue that you are having with a direct employee instead of taking the problem to your direct manager.

When there is no trust, employees will end up gossiping because they feel as though there is no appropriate path to fix their problems.

In my company, we have paved a broad path for our employees to take their problems to the appropriate individual. I have told my team that if they feel like they cannot take their problems to their immediate boss, then take the problems to another leader in the company. If I find that an employee is still not taking their problems up, but rather taking them to the side or down, I will free their future fast. I do not tolerate any sort of gossip because I know that gossip just breeds more gossip.

Lastly, when employees don't feel trusted, their heart cannot connect to meaningful work. Work, in some ways, is a spiritual act. We are meant to work. There is a great reward for hard work. When your heart isn't connected to your work, what is the point?

That's why I love BELAY. We help people, and my employees are changing the world from their own little nook. They feel trusted, and their hearts connect to their mission.

As Paige put it, "I feel like I grow as a leader every day, and I love that. I love how we learn to lead people and be leaders. Period. I think that the company, more than anything, is just doing great things. I love our mission."

HOW TO FIND VIRTUAL EMPLOYEES

WHO WE HIRE

When we first started BELAY, the US job market was faltering on the heels of the 2008 financial crisis, lovingly known as the Great Recession. There were many people around us who were suddenly without work. For that reason, we hired many of our family, friends, and friends of friends.

Now that we are established, we don't hire family and are cautious about the friends we hire. We advertise for virtual team members.

When advertising for openings, we target college-educated, stay-at-home moms or dads with past business or professional experience. This group has been royally marginalized by corporate America. We have found that this niche group of people fit perfectly with our structure because a top priority for them is flexibility in their work. One of the hardest jobs on the planet is being a mom or dad, and for those moms or dads who also need to be making money, we can offer them a great place to work without the typical stressors of an in-office, nine-to-five (or longer) job. They can work when and where they need to so they can continue to be present for their kids.

Another group of people we attract are those who are further along in life and are looking for a meaningful job to fill time. Often people in this group are parents (mostly mothers) of children who are now grown and are either out of the house or on their way out of the house.

Our third major hiring demographic are adult kids of aging parents who have to stay at home to care for them. These people—often in their forties, fifties, sixties, and beyond—are rockstars who can't make it to an office because of circumstances.

HOW WE HIRE

Because BELAY grew so fast, we had to hire on a lot of people quickly. I found that, when hiring senior-level leaders, it was best to hire from within the company rather than going outside of the company to fill those spots. At first, we tried to hire outside people as senior-level employees, but it didn't work out because I felt that they did not align with our culture. They had a hard time understanding our mission. They started politicking. They started gossiping and climbing over other people to look better. I hate that sort of behavior. It tells me that those people are not engaged with what we are doing; they are only out for themselves.

So, I learned my lesson. Now, with few exceptions, I promote from within.

WHAT WE LOOK FOR WHEN HIRING

When we want to fill a new position, we do not write up a traditional job description. Instead, we use something called Key Result Areas (KRAs). I borrowed this term from Dave Ramsey who wrote the *New York Times* best seller called *EntreLeadership*. (More on Dave later!)

Instead of throwing out a dozen or so bullet points of what a position will entail, a KRA tells a potential applicant what it looks like to be successful at the particular position.

So, a typical KRA will say, "You are winning at your job when it looks like this…"

We find that KRAs are better indicators of what a job actually entails and help our applicants understand exactly what it takes to win at their role and satisfy the company.

We just created a new role called "Strategic Partnership Consultant," which is all about helping our clients manage partnerships and build the business. If you would like to see an example of the KRA for our Strategic Partnership Consultant, head over to our website at http://virtualculturebook.com/kra.

SHARPEST TOOL IN THE SHED

We provide tools so that our employees can do the best job possible for us. We give our employees Mac Computers. If they want a PC, they must provide their own, and it must have a high-speed internet connection and a webcam. We also provide them with the best web-based software and applications.

We also provide an in-depth training program for our new employees. Training is vital to offer for any new employee, but it is even more crucial to provide for virtual employees.

Why is that? Imagine getting a job as a virtual employee. Imagine sitting alone at your house and not knowing what to do or where to go for help. If on day one you have no clear plan, you begin to question if this new job was such a good idea after all.

At BELAY, we map out the first month for our leaders and the first two to three weeks for our frontline employees and managers. We map out each day, hour by hour. It is a strict schedule, but we want to make sure new hires understand our culture and what is going to make them successful.

First, we pay for and send them a book and an essay that they are required to read. The book is *EntreLeadership* by Dave Ramsey, and the essay is *"The Servant as Leader"* by Robert Greenleaf. We ask them to give each a thorough read-through. Then we ask them to "net out" and talk about the main points they got out of each book with their manager. We provide an example of a net out on our website at http://virtualculturebook.com/netout.

Next, we give our new employees access to online courses on DigitalChalk that contain videos and lessons. The content ranges across many different topics: there is a welcome message from me, some history about the company, information on how to resolve conflict, the rules of engagement of the company, the appropriate pathways of communication, and even a video about why I hate gossip.

There are also resources in that online course on managing an inbox, email etiquette, time management, owning your calendar before it owns you, and much more. We teach them what is appropriate to say on social media. We talk about our annual summits (all-team face to face meetings) that we offer for our employees and why those summits are important to us. We tell them why we don't do anonymous surveys. We have them complete DiSC profiles (an assessment like Myers-Briggs). We teach them what type of personality they fall under and how to work with people who fall under different personality types. We teach them why we want them to read the things we send them. We also teach our new hires how to be ambassadors for our brand and how to tee up a conversation that might lead to a sale.

We talk about why we share our weekly Highs and Lows on Workplace by Facebook.

We train them on all of the web applications we use. We provide a thorough overview on how to leverage Google Drive, Dropbox, Infusionsoft, Smartsheets, and the myriad of other web-based systems we use. We train them on the specific ways we use to communicate with each other, including email, Instant Messaging, Basecamp, Facebook, and others.

We give our new hires the lowdown on our unique internal

programs. They learn about our Frugal WOW for employees, contractors, clients, and partners, and about another one of our programs that we like to call "Pay It Forward." This program allows employees to donate money to a fund. If something happens to any of our employees—like they get in a car wreck or their dishwasher breaks—we have a Pay It Forward committee that decides when and where to deploy some of the fund money.

We also educate new hires on our equal pay programs and referral bonuses.

Occasionally, we like to pay for outside training programs run by experts. We recently hired Scott Livingston, who writes about and consults on the importance of emotional intelligence and how businesses can leverage emotional intelligence to build deeper relationships with customers.

We love to bring in experts for a day or two who are on the cutting edge so that we can make sure that both our new hires and our longstanding employees are up to date and ready to rock. Housing an expert for a couple of days is great, but I am cautious about inviting long-term consultants into the business. I've always struggled with consultants because I believe that sometimes they are paid to make you sick and then make you well. I will speak to this from personal experience later on in the book.

All of this training helps to keep my employees well aware of what we require of them during their time with us. We like to keep it simple and straightforward.

For Paige, I offered her a ninety-day grace period when she could ask any question over and over and over again as many times as she needed to. She said she wasn't afraid to ask what she considered to be "dumb questions." At first, she said she was nervous to start out in a virtual environment, but the training made her feel confident. I also made sure that she understood that everyone else in the company was happy to answer questions. She found that "everyone was eager to help her." No one told her that something "wasn't [their] job" or that they "didn't have time" for her. Paige quickly realized that we were all there to help her learn how to be the best she could be. We wanted her to be there, and we wanted her to succeed. Same as with every other employee who walks through our virtual door.

Bottom line: Excellent training is important to me. No question about it! It should be a mandate for you as well if you are serious about creating a great onboarding experience.

WHAT MAKES A GOOD VIRTUAL EMPLOYEE?

A good virtual employee embodies eight characteristics...

A good virtual employee is results-oriented and is a motivated self-starter. A good virtual employee is not just at work to punch a time clock and receive a check. A virtual employee gets their work done and feels satisfied when working.

A good virtual employee values working from home and values working hard at home. When I say "home," I do not only mean in their actual house. I just use the phrase "work from home" as a catch-all for all of the places that a virtual employee can work that is not an office. This could mean a coffee shop, a library, or even a coworking space. But, ultimately, a good virtual employee is fine with working independently and outside of a traditional office or group environment. They must also be committed to creating a distraction-free workspace for themselves that they can return to day in and day out.

There are people who value working in a shared space. In fact, there is a group of younger workers that hunger for that collaborative office space. There are people who are just starting off in their careers or who have just moved to a new city and are looking to make friends, so they want to spend their days working around others. As a team, we get together as best we can; we do a lot of fun stuff together, like big dinners, family days, ballgames, etc., but we don't see each other daily, and we don't have weekly or biweekly happy hours. That is just not what this is about. We can't offer that type of environment, so we won't compete against that.

But we do find that there are people who either perpetually prefer working from home or are at a point in their lives that necessitates that they work from home. When you become a parent, have a sick or aging parent, or need flexibility throughout your day, you start to value being closer to home and executing from home.

A good virtual employee values flexibility and autonomy in their work. Often, this requires them to be a natural-born problem solver and critical thinker because there is no one present to hold their hand through every step. In the interview process, we ask open-ended questions to determine candidates' problem-solving abilities and how they think through situations. We love people who can just figure it out!

On that note, a good virtual employee must also adopt a communication style where they are forthcoming and able to correspond clearly and effectively with those around them. In our business, we have to over communicate since we communicate mostly through written word. We all have to be able to parse out exactly what we mean so there isn't much left to interpret! Employees also need to know when to pick up the phone and call!

In my opinion, a great virtual communicator has the ability and desire to see from the perspective of everyone he communicates with. He anticipates what his coworkers will need more clarification on, what questions they may have as they read through material, and which words may not be clear enough. He is sympathetic to his audience, and that makes him more thoughtful and thorough in his communication.

When it came time to getting accustomed to the virtual work world, Paige had to adjust her communication style. She said the communication shift isn't about communicating more, just about communicating differently.

She elaborated, "For instance, sending someone one more email back just to confirm or to say, 'Okay, got it!' Or sending an email just updating someone on the timeline of your project...keeping people in the loop. Just making sure they know you're alive and still working."

Good virtual employees are also normally organized and have great time-management skills. We need our virtual employees to be able to manage their time and put down their phones and close their laptops. We want them to understand boundaries because sometimes working from home blurs the lines.

As with all hiring, it is just as difficult to hire a great virtual employee as it is to hire a great in-office worker. Hiring is a tricky and difficult task to accomplish.

BIG BUT...

You can hedge your risk with hiring virtual employees by keeping in mind an important fact. Studies show that some new graduates want to work in shared spaces. They want face time and social interaction. These types of people, although great, just do not make good virtual employees.

Our hiring managers at BELAY have put together a list of warning signs that we have come to find spell out trouble for virtual employees.

It is a red flag if a virtual employee has no dedicated work-space. Working from home is great because of the freedom it allows, but making sure that you have one space that is free from distraction is important. The office space needs to look and feel professional. For instance, my team has interviewed people over Zoom who had Jack Daniels bottles in the background and raunchy pictures on their walls. We even had someone show up to an interview in a bathrobe! The point is, you aren't going to get hired if your space isn't professional.

We are cautious about hiring employees who lack basic technical skills. Working remotely requires the use of many different applications and tools. Yes, we offer training on those tools, but if an employee is not savvy enough to even figure out how to turn their webcam on, we usually see that as a bad sign.

My hiring team also keeps a close eye on symptoms that reveal a person who is easily distracted or not self-motivated. There are a million things that could distract a virtual employee who is working from home: laundry, dirty dishes, pets that need a lot of attention, and friends who innocently take advantage of your work-from-home status and want to hang out all the time. The list goes on. We need to make sure our people can push those things aside and focus.

The final red flag is also one of the most common: people who want to work virtually as a replacement for childcare. We get a lot of people who think they can kill two birds with one stone by working and taking care of their kids right from the comfort of their living room. This is just not the case, regardless of how many parenting magazines say otherwise! We want you to work from home to hang out with your kids more, sure. But we don't want our virtual employees hanging out with their kids while they work. Anyone who knows anything about parenting knows just how much of a disaster that usually turns out to be!

GOOD EMPLOYEE, BAD EMPLOYEE

In the end, the thing that makes or breaks most businesses are the leaders. There is only so much you can do to make sure you have the right employees. The most important thing you must have is a great leader. If you have a great leader, many parts of the bad employees can be excused or even corrected.

What makes a great leader? The answer is many things, but I believe it comes down to one primary thing: communicating the why.

When employees don't know the why, they begin to wonder, "Why am I here?" If you leave it to your employees to answer that question for themselves, the answers can get pretty negative very fast.

That is why you must communicate the why. The why trumps the how, what, when, and where. If your employees know the why, they can fill in the blanks on the how, what, when, and where when their leader is not around.

LEADER ON THE MOUNTAIN

Our company is named BELAY after the verb "belay." In our case, "belay" comes from the world of rock climbing. The person on the ground attached to the climber by a rope is the one who belays. The belayer acts as a safeguard who, by using his or her own body weight, will catch the climber if he falls. The belayer enables the climber to climb as high as he can without needing to fear falling.

That is what we do at BELAY: we act as that safeguard on the ground, enabling our clients to climb higher. The belayer helps the climber achieve the summit. The belayer serves in a support role. More practically stated, our vision at BELAY is to help our clients achieve their vision.

This climbing theme is also present in how I think about leadership. There is an awesome and inspirational quote by a famous climber by the name of René Daumal. He wrote,

"You cannot stay on the summit forever; you have to come down again. So why bother in the first place? Just this: what is above knows what is below, but what is below does not know what is above. One climbs, one sees. One descends, one sees no longer, but one has seen. There is an art of conducting oneself in the lower regions by the memory of what one saw higher up. When one can no longer see, one can at least still know."

To me, Daumal is saying that those people who climb mountains have an advantage over those who stand at the bottom of a mountain looking up at it. Although someone who has stood on top of a summit must come down, he at least carries with him the knowledge of what it was like to be at the top. He gets to take that knowledge and share it with all of those people down below who never have and never will climb that mountain.

That is how I feel about what it is like to be a leader. A leader has the knowledge and vision from standing on top of that summit that his employees may not have. That is why the leader must communicate the why to his employees; they can't know themselves, so they have to be told.

When a leader articulates the why, he is metaphorically leading his employees to the top of the summit so they can understand without needing to climb it themselves. It is just as much my job to climb up the mountain as it is to climb back down.

CHAPTER 4

LEADERSHIP IS A STEWARDSHIP

—

Over the course of almost twenty years, I have learned about the principle of leadership as stewardship from my pastor, Andy Stanley. I've taken what I've learned from him and applied it to how I live my life and how I lead others.

I lead by the principle of stewardship. To me, stewardship means that I was given something to take care of, and now I am held accountable for its well-being. Stewardship is time bound. I have met owners and CEOs of companies who act like they are going to be in charge forever. But, of course, that is never true. One thing I know for sure is that everyone is going to die at some point.

My wife and I look at our role at BELAY as temporary. For the season of time that we hold our positions, we are responsible for BELAY's well-being and the well-being of all of the people it houses. When our season is over, we hope to hand it off to someone in the best possible condition; we want BELAY to be here for our children and grandchildren and beyond.

I believe leaders who think of themselves as stewards are the ones worth following.

I have always wanted to be a leader worth following. The desire started small. When I was young, I told my parents that I wanted to own my own company. My longing to lead manifested itself throughout my life in bigger ways. On the soccer field in high school and college, I was the captain and the goalkeeper. I set the offense in motion, and I was the last person to keep that ball from hitting the net. I was also involved in student government in college. Right out of the gate, I threw myself into the role and got promoted to lead others. Over time, I developed my personal why for why I liked to lead people.

WHAT'S YOUR WHY?

There are days that being a leader is tough, but that personal why keeps you going.

My personal why is that I love to watch people develop. I like to have a small hand in their growth. I've been intentional in creating a company where people feel like they can grow and where they are pushed to explore the possibilities of their growth. That, to me, is what stewardship and leadership is all about: a responsibility to help people grow.

For instance, as a sales guy at heart, it is my duty to steward the growth of my sales team. Each member of my sales team knows that if they have a prospect that they want me to call in, I will. I will work to advance the ball for them, and I will work my hardest to get in and close that deal.

I usually don't use war analogies, but there is one that I'm partial to: I like being in the trenches. I will not be up on the hill behind my troops, looking at the enemy through binoculars. I will always be in the trenches with my team, helping them in whatever way I can—whether they see me or not.

My ability to steward my employees was put to the test last year when we decided to consolidate our five companies into one. My wife and I stood up and told our employees, "Follow us. There is a new day coming, and it is an excellent day for our company. You have to trust us."

They did trust us and followed us through the consolidation process.

I think they followed because they felt they could hold me accountable as a leader to uphold the ideas that I championed. That accountability is, by the way, essential in a good leader. If I decide on a course of action, then I am held accountable for it. If I tell my employees that we need to live by a certain value, then I must live by that very same value.

ADULTING AT WORK

Do everything you can to let your team know that you trust them even when you can't see them, even if that means you have to belabor the point over and over. Don't miss this: adults need to be reminded that they are trusted!

Speaking of belaboring the point, make sure to cast your vision as frequently as possible so that everyone understands the trajectory of the company. The why is more important than the what, how, and when.

You have to be more communicative—to the point of over communicating—with virtual employees. Internally, we call this "breaking the threshold of communication." For example, let's say that Mary is going to come on as an employee at BELAY. I am going to spend the first ninety days communicating more frequently with her. I will call her and IM her more often. Even the style of communication with her will be more thorough; I won't use abbreviations (especially internal abbreviations) as much, and I will make sure to give her more information in each interaction than I normally would.

There will be a point where Mary will tell me, "Okay, cool I've got it." That's the point that I call "breaking the threshold of communication." It is the moment where Mary or any other employee tells me they don't need my guidance as much anymore.

Don't sit there and worry about what your employees are doing day to day. Don't wonder if they are really doing their job. Trust that they are. Look for the results.

Lead by example. If you have a policy where you require everyone to bug off of their email by 6:00 p.m. but you are sending emails at 10:00 p.m., then you are not leading by example. This type of behavior does not bode well in a virtual environment. You must walk the walk!

Follow through on what you believe. My wife and I must often make tough decisions regarding the business. Recently, a company that wanted to use our service approached us, but we felt very uncomfortable with their ethos. We had to tell them no. We felt that because we are stewards of the brand, the employees, the business, and the values we espouse, that particular partnership would have led us in a direction where we did not want to go.

So, despite the fact that saying no kept us from closing a sale, we wanted to remain loyal to our beliefs. I have found that when we hold our values close, we can use them as a filter in our decision-making. Looking to my core values has helped me make challenging decisions. Because Shannon and I believed so strongly that we wanted to run BELAY with values in mind, we set out to define our values so that everyone in the business knows where we stand.

Making sure we got those values down was crucial to me. In the summer of 2012, Shannon and I got our team together in a cabin in the North Georgia mountains. At the time, there were twelve of us. Our goal for the weekend was to figure out BELAY's values.

I said, "Everybody, get a bunch of sheets of paper and start writing down one word that represents our business."

Between the twelve of us, we had around three hundred sheets of paper. Then we began to consolidate. We'd stack words on top of each other or underneath each other based on how they related.

Five values bubbled up: God, team, passion, gratitude,

and vision. We adopted the sixth one in 2016: fun. We added it after we realized that we always try to make things fun for our employees. Once we figured out these values, we sat down and brainstormed how to express them. The subtext of what we do came out of that. A word to the wise: your company values are not set in stone! Give yourself permission to develop your values as your company matures.

These six values make up our culture. I feel that my job as CEO is to defend the company's culture forever, like a mama bear would her cubs. I'm naturally good at it because I can read people really well.

Lastly, do not overlook the importance of physical, face-to-face meetings from time to time. Most people hunger for personal connection, and work is no exception. For that reason, although I dedicate myself to the virtual model, I can't be so dedicated that I am unwilling to be flexible in the interests of my employees. When you starve employees—either virtual employees or in-office employees who work in the cubicle next to their boss—of face-to-face, personal interaction, you end up isolating them. I do not want to do that.

We decided early that because we were a virtual company, we were going to have to work extra hard to get in front of our employees. That is why we organize summits and other various outings and events for our corporate team, so that they can interact with my family and me. We have found that getting together only enhances the virtual relationship.

For our contractors, we need to fulfill that interaction in different ways because they are often not located in the Atlanta metro. We have been testing ways to promote meetups. We encourage our employees to get together to talk, collaborate, connect, build connections, and get that necessary dose of personal contact. Lunch is on us!

Our contactors have told us that they appreciate the initiative, and a lot of them have developed personal connections with each other that wouldn't have otherwise happened.

MY GUIDING PRINCIPLES OF LEADERSHIP
LET LIFE HAPPEN

First, employees' lives matter. Period. I dislike leaders and owners that treat their employees as cogs. Leaders forget that their employees are real people and have problems and things going on in their personal lives. There are a million things that people suffer through every day, and they bring that burden into their job whether leaders like that or not. Employees may be dealing with a serious illness or quietly going through a divorce. Everyone is dealing with something. It's true of the leader. It's true of the contractors. It's true of the guy sorting the mail in the mailroom.

I know leaders who tell their employees to leave their issues at the door. That is irresponsible. As a leader, you have to let life happen. Leaders forget that these people work to advance the cause of their brand—they dedicate their days to contributing to the success of the business, and that is important to remember.

Because I am concerned with what my employees are privately going through, I require everyone to use video chat instead of phone calls. It is easy to miss those silent struggles if you can't see someone's face and look into their eyes. If I am video-conferencing with an employee and I notice something is off, there is no chance I won't ask them what is wrong. Often, bringing out their struggles helps them to overcome them, or at least feel like both me and BELAY as a whole are supportive.

TRUST TRUMPS SUSPICION

Operate on the basis of trust, not suspicion. I've mentioned this topic previously, but I want to reiterate its importance because it is one of my favorite topics to talk about with people who are building new companies, especially if those companies operate in a virtual environment.

It is human nature to default to being suspicious of someone if you can't see them. I get it. There are some bad people in the world. But I think that it is not true of most people; most people in this world are good. The media will tell you otherwise. Our parents will, too. They've raised us to believe that if a person is a stranger, then that person is bad. I just don't live my life that way. So, my modus operandi is to trust. I assume the best of people.

I make sure that this sentiment comes out in our Rules of Engagement that I require all of my employees to read. The bottom line is this: we want our employees to choose to trust rather than to be suspicious of each other. Employees operating in virtual cultures have to fight the natural inclination to be distrustful.

For example, if my assistant, Paige, misses a deadline, I assume that she missed the deadline for a legitimate reason. Maybe she was working on something else. Maybe she was waiting on someone else for a component of the project to come through. I am going to give her the opportunity to give me a good reason—and I trust that she has one—rather than assuming she missed that deadline out of spite or laziness or whatever else. So far, this has worked wonderfully for me, and it can for you as well.

DELEGATION IS THE NAME OF THE GAME

If a leader does not delegate and empower his employees, he cannot scale. I learned to delegate so that I could continue to lead and do the things I am good at so the business grows.

I love sales, and I'm really good at it. I remember for the first eighteen months into our business, I sold every contract. But there was a point where I told myself, "I've got to get out of the way of the business because it is growing quicker than I can sell." For that reason, I decided to delegate sales to someone else.

The same was true with my wife, Shannon, and our bookkeeping. Both she and I are not great bookkeepers. She was spending so much time trying to take account of our corporate finances, and there were several screw-ups and instances where we had to pay someone to fix problems we created. We decided to delegate.

Because of the quick growth of the company, Shannon and I had to learn to delegate fast. We have found that there are two rules leaders should consider when delegating.

The first: delegate the things you hate doing. Shannon hated accounting, so we got ourselves an accountant!

The second: delegate the things that anyone could do. What does this mean? Well, for instance, I love sales, yet I still delegated that role. Why? Because I knew that (almost) anyone I hired as a salesperson could get the job done. Meanwhile, I could spend more of my time doing the jobs that only I could do: leading the company, networking, representing our brand, protecting our culture, and casting a vision.

At BELAY, we have designed a Delegation Matrix to help leaders understand where and when they should delegate. We know leaders often feel overwhelmed by all of the responsibilities piled on their desks, so the matrix helps them to see that they can pass along many of those tasks to their team. This way, they can focus on the tasks that only they can do. Focus is crucial. Leaders like Warren Buffett and Bill Gates consistently bring up focus as an ability that makes leaders great...check out our Delegation Matrix at the end of this chapter to learn how to bring more focus to your role!

INVEST IN THE US

Contributing positively to the US economy is my last principle of leadership. While commerce today is very global, as an American citizen, I have always been a firm believer in my duty as a business leader to do my part in upholding the health of the US economy. As I mentioned before, we started the company in 2010, and at the time, the unemployment rate was at almost 10 percent. Although the economy is in a much better place currently, my goal to contribute to domestic financial health has only become more important. Seven years later, this goal is a key differentiator for us.

STRONG CORE

Each member of our corporate team is required to live in the Atlanta metro. Limiting our geographic search for candidates was a big decision for us. Ultimately, though, it was an important decision to make. I firmly believed that I needed to have a more personal connection with my core group of people. There are times when a leader needs to circle the wagons and sit down to have a face-to-face when running a business. I admit, there are some times where Zoom just won't do.

Just last week, I got our leadership team down to the beach. We made a silly but awesome music video to send out to our employees, and we had a blast making it. After, we went out and had food and drinks and talked about our lives, and we played a game where we said something we liked about the person sitting to our right. There were tears at the table. As I looked around at my team, I had this overwhelming feeling of happiness.

I thought to myself, "Man, I'm so thankful that I can work with such incredible people like this. I will charge up a hill for these people sitting around me."

I want them to feel the same way for each other; in fact, I need them to feel that way. But I believe that we can only get there through the very personal interactions we have face-to-face—like the ones we had that night.

I acknowledge that I have set limitations on my virtual workforce. Some may think I am a hypocrite for having such limitations. But at the time when I was organizing my company, I believed keeping my corporate team in Atlanta was the best call—and I still believe that. It saves me a fortune on travel when we have to circle the wagons when making big decisions. It is important to me that management and leadership meet when making life-altering decisions that might affect hundreds of people.

But that only takes into account the top of a company. The rest of the employees can be located as far away from the epicenter as they want.

How can I keep my atmosphere collaborative with my employees distributed all over the country?

First, I use technology to keep us all communicating. At BELAY, we use Slack, Workplace by Facebook, Google Hangouts, and other forms of instant messaging. But the number one best weapon we use is a webcam. Web calling is massively important to me and my team.

Webcams can bridge the virtual gap a lot better than a phone call can. Leveraging the power of the webcam is imperative when running a virtual company; I love the power of video, especially when I want to hit home on a potent point. Instead of sending out a long-winded memo, hopping on the webcam is so much more effective. For instance, not too long ago, Shannon and I realized we were looking at the wrong metric in defining our next fiscal year. Because I wouldn't be able to get in front of the team for a couple of months, I set up a video conference to let them know we were switching things up. I was able to get my point across exactly how and when I needed to.

When I asked Paige what she found to be easier than expected when getting used to working virtually, she said, "Using video conference. They are the norm now." Not only has video helped her professionally, but her team has used it to build their personal relationships with each other, too. Video has helped her to build a community of friends. According to Paige, "Two of my coworkers are my best friends now." They even set up video conferences where they just work together in silence! They have even started using Zoom to host a Bible study group outside of work!

Paige says web calls are an important indicator of client success, too. "If our clients choose not to connect, not to do web calls, that just does not bode well for them because they won't succeed. They can't succeed. People won't be happy if they're not connecting with other people."

CULTURE FOR COLLABORATION

Paige also spoke to me about how much she loved BELAY Buddies, a program we have set up to connect our employees with each other and get them used to working over video.

"We're assigned one person who we don't know very well, and we set up a fifteen-minute Zoom call just to chat," explains Paige. "We talk about family, friends, struggles, hobbies. It's great! I never anticipated making friends in a virtual job, but they're some of my dearest friends now. BELAY and the people here foster that. Bryan and Shannon take initiatives to emphasize personal connections."

At BELAY, we have something called a Virtual Happy Hour. It is exactly what it sounds like: the whole team sits in front of the computer wherever they may be with a drink in hand. We have a blast during those sessions.

I've mentioned our strict no gossip rule and no anonymous surveys rule before, but I want to mention them here again because they are both major contributing factors in a collaborative workspace. As for the no gossip rule, of course, I want my employees to talk about their lives with each other and to talk about the struggles that they face both professionally and personally. However, I do not want my employees bringing problems sideways or down, or talking poorly about a colleague. That is inexcusable. As for the no anonymous survey rule, creating an environment where my employees can own their words is a great way for them to open up and speak truthfully to me and each other. Truth enables collaboration. No question about it.

On the topic of owning your words and speaking the truth, at BELAY, we believe in running towards difficult conversations, not away from them. If we avoid those hard conversations, it leads to grudges. Negative feelings stew. I always start hard conversations simply. I say things like, "I didn't like it when you did X," or "Please don't do X again," or "I like it when you do X this way."

Paige recalled a time when we had to have a hard conversation. "One time, we had a corporate event, and the guest speaker went way over his time, and it put us behind schedule." She remembered that I pulled her aside and said, "This is bad. We need to fix this. I do not like when we go over schedule." Paige said it only took that one time for her to learn that about me. Now, she makes sure that guest speakers know their time limit.

VALUES FOR COLLABORATION

The last point I want to make about creating a collaborative virtual environment is about values. As I mentioned previously, at BELAY, we run our company based on values. These values make up our culture, which in turn drives our mission. Because we have distributed employees, we want to make sure that they understand our values and have a way of personally connecting with them. So, we began an initiative to make sure this was the case.

Paige is in charge of the program. She calls every single one of our corporate employees once a year and tests them on BELAY's values. She makes seventy calls in three days! Her goal is to make sure every employee knows them by heart and can talk about at least one area in the company where they see that value.

When I was interviewing Paige for this book, I said, "Pop quiz! What are our values?"

She laughed because I had turned the tables on her. Here's what she said:

"**God** is our Number One. He gets the glory, not us. We believe that He brought us here and He provided this world for us. He called us to serve other people, to be, as He says, His hands and His feet. I just love that because you don't have to be working in a church to feel like you're accomplishing that mission, and when we put others before ourselves and treat them better, people feel that and gravitate towards us. At my old job, we had to do deceitful things, and it felt very icky. Honoring Him puts an upside-down situation right-side up. At BELAY, you don't have to be a Christian by any means; it's just something you have to respect. It just means that you are on board to serve other people.

"**Team.** We're all in this together. We run to our problems, challenges, and opportunities. We never say, 'That's not my job.' We do love to help each other, but we also know how to turn that off. If I am busy and can't help my teammates, we are taught how to say no gracefully. That is just part of being on a team, recognizing that you have too much to do to go around helping. [Bryan] passed around an article by Richard Branson that says that we should use 'we' instead of 'they,' and that has changed how we talk in meetings.

"**Passion.** Passion encompasses both service and leadership. Our passion is to serve others, which demonstrates our leadership.

"**Vision.** We are leaders in our industry. We refuse to accept the status quo. We have the vision of what can be. I love this one because even though we want to honor God and have fun, we also want to be the best, work the hardest, have the greatest reputation, and we want people to say good things about us. We want to be the brightest, the smartest, and the quickest. We want to rise to the top. We want to be a successful company that everyone benefits from.

"**Gratitude.** That's huge. I don't think a day goes by that I don't hear from you about how grateful you are for me. It was so opposite of the culture that I came from. I hardly ever heard the word 'thanks.' I don't know if any other CEO practices gratitude like how you do. You also acknowledge when you call me after 6:00 p.m. and I'm making dinner. Your gratitude makes me want to work harder because I know you appreciate it. Showing gratitude keeps people happy and the little things you hear day in and day out go a long way. When gratitude drives our actions, it reminds people that you are not alone. You thank those people that have helped you get to where you are."

When I asked Paige about our culture at BELAY, she paused for a moment, and then smiled, "**Fun!**" Fun is our sixth value. Paige said, "We don't take ourselves too seriously...seriously. That is a new one, but it was added because it was always an underlying thing. We put a huge emphasis on our events, and we do virtual happy hours. You are the one that puts on these huge events. We're like, that is going to cost ten thousand dollars; you're like, 'Let's do it.' We have to hold you back on the fun sometimes! On calls, we make things fun. We talk about people and congratulate them for their successes. We don't want anything ever to be dry or mind-numbing. We recognize that when we ask people to join meetings, they are taking time away from their families, and we understand that family is the most important thing, and so if we are going to do that, we should at least make it fun and worth your while and not something that you dread going to. We all work hard and play hard...we all just have a good time."

Paige wanted me to add one more thing: "Anybody who wants to go virtual should definitely implement some of these things—or all of them—in order to make for a happy company. Not to say that it's perfect and that everybody ends their day happy all of the time. But we work hard, and we deeply care about what we do."

Couldn't have said it better myself.

HOW TO TRAIN A VIRTUAL EMPLOYEE

I've already gone into the more granular side of our new employee training, but it's important to me that I talk about the philosophies behind the training. I mentioned before that we supplement our training program with *EntreLeadership* by Dave Ramsey and *The Servant as Leader* by Robert Greenleaf. These two works pretty much summarize what I'm all about and what I want my employees to get out of working with me.

I love Robert Greenleaf. When he published his essay in 1977, his concept of servant leadership was groundbreaking. In my opinion, forty years later, it still is. If you ask most people who created the idea of servant leadership, they'd say Robert Greenleaf first, and then second to him, Christ.

I was first introduced to *The Servant as Leader* when an ex-boss of mine (whom I admire) said that reading it changed him as a leader.

I thought, "Well, that is a pretty bold statement, and I like this guy, so I should probably pay attention to this servant leadership stuff."

So, I did, and boy did it change me, and it led me to my personal why.

When I worked for that boss, I was young—about twenty-nine years old and full of a real passion for leading. I was always bothering him, begging him to let me take the reins on a project here and there.

I told him, "I want to lead. Please promote me; please give me some people to manage."

One day, I think he was so fed up with my pestering him that he asked me a question that changed everything for me. We were going up on an escalator at a hotel in downtown Atlanta and I was, again, asking him when I could get a project to lead.

He turned to me. He looked me dead in the eye and calmly said, "Why do you want to lead?"

The question took me aback. It was such a simple, honest question, but I had no answer. I had never even considered why I wanted to lead, I had always just felt a burning need.

I told him, "I don't know."

He nodded his head and informed me that I needed to develop my why before we could begin our discussion about leadership.

Although it was kind of brutal, I wasn't upset; he was dead on.

So, I went on a quest to find out why I wanted to lead people. It wasn't easy, but by the end, I realized that I too wanted to be a servant leader. I personally love to watch people develop, and I work to steward each of my employees into the person they want to become; both personally and professionally.

That was my why. I started from that basic desire and have since worked every day to keep that why close at heart.

I also have my employees read *EntreLeadership*. It was an impactful book for me and my wife. In it, we discovered a lot of principles that we now use to carry our business forward. We hope that our employees will take in those principles and actively work to look for where those principles show themselves in the company. I want them to stop and think, "Oh, I see how that principle plays out here."

The most crucial part of our training program is ensuring

our employees understand the underlying principles upon which BELAY was built.

Let's dive into the more granular pieces of the training program: the how behind the why. As mentioned before, training includes mandatory reading, online tutorials, and a series of videos employees have to watch. For anyone new who is coming in, his or her first three weeks are structured hour by hour.

We created an extensive training program using Digital-Chalk where we have an extensive network of resources that our employees can access.

We spend a lot of time training our virtual employees about how to prioritize. Like I said before, time management and prioritization skills are key. Imagine you are a new employee working for a virtual company. First day on the job, you are sitting in your house with no idea what you are supposed to do next. It's irresponsible of any organization to not have a robust, structured training plan in place for the first couple of weeks. Virtual companies have to provide that. If one of my employees is sitting at home, looking around, and asking what to do, that is on me.

There are some people out there who assume that somehow, by osmosis, they are going to have a great employee who is just going to get it and jump right in. Unless good hires are properly trained, they don't make good employees. We have customers who hire our virtual contractors and say, "We'll just let them figure it out." No. They have a responsibility to train their employees. They need to be stewarded.

A lot of employees in a virtual environment feel like they have to do everything—and all at once. They feel like all of their work is of equal value or equal priority. In reality, it isn't. I teach my employees a simple trick to rank duties so they don't feel overwhelmed.

Open up a Word document and write out three lists: "Must," "Should," and "Could." Ask yourself what you must do today and list out one to three things. Then ask what you should do and list out one to three things. Lastly, ask yourself what you could do today. Fill that list out as well. This helps me prioritize my day. Find an example at http://virtualculturebook.com/mustshouldcould.

Part of teaching people how to prioritize is teaching them when they should solve a problem versus when they should bring the problem to their manager.

My rule of thumb is that unless there is an emergency, I will not solve my employees' problems for them. If they call me or email me and say, "We have a problem," I think, "No, *you* have a problem." I want to teach people how to solve their own problems and become leaders in their own right.

When one of my employees has a problem, they should come to me with that problem only if they've already thought through three potential ways to solve it. I tell them, "Don't come to me with problems; come to me with solutions." I will happily sit there and talk about how to navigate the problem via the solutions that they bring to me.

The more you make them think through their problems over time, the less they will come to you. The more they understand how I, as the leader, think through things, the more they understand how they should think through things.

That is how I steward the business. Eventually, I won't be here anymore, but the business can still be here because the leaders and the employees running it know how to.

Three years into starting our business, my family and I took a much-deserved, month-long vacation. There weren't any issues; the business could run itself because I had stewarded my employees to be leaders. I had empowered them to make decisions for themselves based on how I taught them to solve problems.

I only had one small problem to deal with during that month-long vacation. I solved it sitting in a hot tub looking at the Tetons. My employees wanted us to have that vacation, and they knew we deserved it, so they figured out how to solve problems by themselves. It worked out. That was a very real reward for me.

People don't start businesses to become slaves to them, but most end up that way. I will not be a slave to the business. It has a rightful place in my life, but I will never be indebted to it. That's why it was so important that I teach my employees how to prioritize, lead, trust, and think for themselves.

BELAY'S DELEGATION MATRIX

We designed the Delegation Matrix to help our employees become better stewards of their responsibilities. I designed it with a friend of mine because he was struggling with delegation. We offer it as a free tool on our website! Find it at http://virtualculturebook.com/matrix.

CHAPTER 5

MYTH BUSTING

———

Before we get any further, I want to bust some myths (in chapter 2, I also refer to them as stigmas) associated with virtual organizations. I had a different idea of what I wanted this chapter to look like, but as I was developing this section, I had an experience that I thought was so important that I had to address it.

In January of 2017, Shannon and I decided we wanted to elevate our team to a new level. BELAY continued to grow fast and be recognized for our epic culture through numerous awards; we were doing great, but we wanted to explore how we could do better. We wanted someone to belay BELAY. So, we decided to hire consultants to come in to teach us strategies to achieve that goal. We admire the

Table Group, led by Pat Lencioni, the best-selling author of *The Five Dysfunctions of a Team*, and so we decided to hire them to help us develop as leaders.

We signed up for a year-long engagement and had a great few months interacting with our personal consultant from the Table Group, a man named Hrishi Baskaran. Hrishi taught us some great tools (which I will chronicle later on in this chapter), and we felt proud to have partnered with them. It was also a cool experience for Hrishi because we were the Table Group's first all-virtual client.

Not surprisingly to me, all of their methods and strategies for their nonvirtual clients translated beautifully into our team. We were rocking and rolling.

That is until Pat Lencioni wrote up an article detailing his feelings about how virtual teams "don't really work." He said a lot of stuff, but the thing that stood out to me was his claim that if you work in a virtual team, it is likely that the leadership doesn't take their jobs seriously and doesn't realize the challenges ahead of them.

That really hit me hard. How could he possibly say that about anyone? How could that be assumed with one of his clients? How could he just assume that about me?

I was shocked.

I was bummed. I am a big Lencioni fan!

And, I'll admit it...I was pissed. I mean, I was paying the Table Group a lot of money (in my young company's eyes) to consult with our leadership team—and this was how he truly felt?

I sent an email to Hrishi about my concerns. I told him that in my eyes, Lencioni's post came across as slightly hostile to my employees and to virtual companies and teams everywhere. I felt like there was likely no way to continue to work with the Table Group based on this assumption. How could I possibly continue to get counsel from a company where the well-known, public leader appeared to be antagonistic to the type of culture we created and wanted to enhance? Truth be told, I was at a boiling point of others trying to delegitimize our very legitimate company simply because we are all-virtual.

Hrishi acknowledged my concerns, and we met up to talk via web call.

During our discussion, I made this clear to him: I believed any leader, author, or speaker who puts his head in the sand about virtual teams, virtual companies, or virtual cultures is ignoring the tsunami that is quickly coming for them. I pointed to the sheer number of employees requesting or demanding to work in a virtual capacity. I pointed to the future. I pointed to facts. I pointed out that virtual teams are here to stay. Hrishi was great on the call and listened to me fume.

Bottom line: this experience hit home for me. I know that there are entrenched myths and stigmas about virtual companies, but through this ordeal, I experienced them head-on. I fight against virtual or remote headwinds every single day, and I will continue to do so because I do believe that it is the future of the workplace. To not embrace the growing request of employees for a remote/virtual opportunity is simply resisting the inevitable.

My struggle with the ordeal was that I really liked Lencioni and the work that he and his team produced. Our team actually reads and implements a lot of his ideas. I wanted to give him the benefit of the doubt because I think his opinions were born from the fact that he had never witnessed a good example of a well-run, all-virtual company. Fortunately, Hrishi was able to set up a meeting for us to meet Pat, who invited me and Shannon to his offices in San Francisco to talk more about BELAY's all-virtual culture.

Pat is a student of healthy organizational cultures. His

personality is absolutely infectious. He asked numerous questions about how we make BELAY work, what our team dynamics are like, and how often we are meeting virtually and face-to-face. He also addressed his article head on, as his experience with a virtual organization was vastly different than how we operate BELAY. He was quick to listen and quick to call out the comparisons. And here's the funny part tied to a happy ending: Pat said our two companies are very similar in culture! All it took was setting the word "virtual" aside and objectively looking at the company cultures we have built. It was a blast of a meeting!

All that to say, we're thrilled with the Table Group: Pat, Amy, Hrishi, and their whole team. Buy all of Pat's books for your team, implement his ideas, and thank me later.

DEBUNKING MYTHS

Here, I want to lend my voice to address some of the most common stigmas that I hear from people about virtual cultures.

MYTH #1: RELATIONSHIPS SUFFER BECAUSE THERE ARE NO PHYSICAL INTERACTIONS

False.

Working virtually actually makes the relationship sweeter. There is nothing better than when you develop a rapport with someone online and then you get to hang out with him or her in real life. It makes that business connection more meaningful, and it enhances your experience.

I have had many opportunities present themselves because I took the time to go see someone and we jelled in person. In sales, people buy from people they like. Of course, I rub some people the wrong way, but I think people like me for the most part. It's beneficial to me because people like to work with people they like.

Another great benefit to a virtual organization is that our inside sales team doesn't need to spend days on airplanes and nights in hotels. We sell virtual services, so if you think about it, if I have to come to you to close a deal, I've defeated the purpose of my business.

MYTH #2: VIRTUAL MEETINGS AREN'T PRODUCTIVE

False.

We make our meetings very productive. I can point directly to the success of BELAY to prove that point; we wouldn't be growing so rapidly and winning awards if we weren't out there grinding.

To make our meetings productive, we send out our meeting agenda ahead of time. We find that when everyone is literally and figuratively on the same page, we can all get where we are going together.

We also have instituted a practice called "lightning rounds" at the beginning of meetings. In the lightning round, each person has a couple of minutes to update everyone on what they are doing. In the lightning round, we don't allow anyone to ask questions. This exercise is just a time for people to get information out. We do a deeper dive later in the meeting, but this practice orients us. Everyone loves lightning rounds because they get their designated time to speak without interruption. We joke that there should be more lightning, less thunder!

We also do something called "Fist of Five." We use this practice when surveying the team. Fist of Five helps us get a read on how people feel about proposed ideas. After the proposal is introduced, we count to three, and everyone holds out their hands with zero to five fingers. Zero fingers mean "No way!" Five fingers mean "Let's do it!"

During our meetings, we "hunt elephants" (don't worry, it's not as violent as it sounds). We do not like when someone talks around the elephant in the room during a meeting. So, if we sense that someone is not addressing the problem head-on, we call them out on it! We encourage them to hunt that elephant!

We also have a "TSA rule": if you see something, say something. It is important to me that if a member of my leadership team sees something going on, they bring it up. I implore them to do that even if that something exists in a part of the business that they are not involved with. Some employees might feel bad because they don't want to step on anyone's toes. I don't care! If there is a problem, say something! Call it out!

We "welcome the contrarian." If everyone in the room is in agreement about an idea, we give our employees permission to explore weaknesses that might have gone overlooked. We want our decisions to be weapons-grade. We want them to thoroughly beat up all accepted ideas from all known angles because we believe conflict (if done well) produces incredible results.

We refuse to go on mute on web calls or conference calls. The mute button kills meeting efficiency. When you go on mute, it is a limiting factor in getting out what needs to be said. It prevents conversation from flowing. The mute button keeps us from having a healthy back and forth, and for that reason, we ban it from my virtual meetings. Trust me on this: don't mute unless you absolutely have to. I've only ever allowed muting when there was a latency issue for someone that was ruining the call for everyone else or the occasional dog bark or a busy barista.

Lastly, we have something called "Z methodology." Every member of my team completed a Myers-Briggs test on my request. I thought it was important for everyone to take that test so that we had a baseline assessment about what type of personality everyone came to the table with. In Z methodology, we play to the strengths of personality types when making a decision. We give everyone the facts, and then ask them how they would solve the problem. Then we make the decision about how we are going to solve the issue.

MYTH #3: VIRTUAL MEETINGS ARE LESS EFFICIENT

Honestly, I've worked in virtual and nonvirtual companies, and I know it is true that virtual meetings are more efficient because we get stuff done in the allotted time of the Zoom call. We are more tactical. We don't sit around a table all day killing time in a meeting. We want to get back to our lives. We are there to work, and that is what we do.

This efficiency is a major win for leaders!

MYTH #4: ORGANIZATIONS WITHOUT AN OFFICE AREN'T MAKING DOUGH

F-a-l-s-e.

This has been a pet peeve of mine for a long time. I find that when I'm around other business owners (mostly guys), they feel like their office gives them status. They act like the grander the office, the more important they are; the more successful they are, the more money they have. For me, I just don't equate office to status, and I think most employees don't perceive it that way, either.

In fact, when they hear that I don't have an office, they look at me sideways and say something like, "Well, you can't be a legitimate business because you don't have an office!"

To that, I like to say, "I bet I have a healthier bottom line than you do. I'm doing things you wish you could do because I have the cash. All your office does is suck cash from your net profit. If you didn't have an office and if you managed your money well, I guarantee you would have a healthier bottom line, too."

WHEN YOU ASSUME, YOU LOSE

When you assume and fall prey to stereotypes and myths,

you lose out on the opportunity to have a meaningful virtual culture.

HAPPY EMPLOYEE FORMULA

Virtual employees are happier than non-virtual employees. I can say that because BELAY is the proof. We are number one in best culture this year according to *Entrepreneur Magazine*. We are the heavyweight champion of the world right now in regard to company culture. We are also virtual. I'm not saying that employees in an office can't be happy...they can. But we've proven that virtual employees can be the happiest.

HAPPY EMPLOYEES LEAD TO HAPPY CUSTOMERS

If you have employees who are passionate about their job, are happy to get up and work every day, are able to work from wherever they want, are treated like adults, and are trusted, you will have a very happy employee and a very happy customer. Everyone has his or her own story of calling into a major cable provider or a major airline and having a nightmare interaction with a miserable customer service rep. Those reps aren't happy, and they transfer that frustration to the customer.

We set ourselves up for success when we create a virtual

environment that makes our people happy. We give them access to superb resources, we have fantastic benefits, we pay them well, and they get to work from their back deck. They have a meaningful why. They do meaningful work that makes them happy.

We get new employees coming into the company and asking if this is for real all of the time. They are really saying, "I really like this place. Please, God, let this be real." They don't believe it when we tell them that they will be happy because they are coming to us from corporate America. They go through a period of detoxing from that environment.

HOUSTON, WE HAVE A SOLUTION

The customer wins when you go virtual.

That has become a part of our mission, too.

We want our customers to climb higher, and we know that only happens when you have happy employees.

That is the reason why people still eat at Chick-fil-A despite the stance and personal beliefs of their leadership. The employees who work there are genuinely happy and care about what they do, and that good feeling gets transferred to the customer.

I can't tell you how many times I've been to Chick-fil-A, thanked an employee for helping me out, and heard, "Of course, my pleasure." I can tell that they actually mean it.

INTERACTIONS WITH CUSTOMERS DON'T HAVE TO BE FACE-TO-FACE TO BE MEANINGFUL AND PERSONAL

At BELAY, when we want to have a meaningful interaction with one of our customers, we don't have to see them face-to-face. I can ask a challenging question over Zoom and plainly see their reaction. I can still watch for all of the implicit body language signs. I can still ask tough questions like, "How are we serving you? What can we do better? Are we doing enough? Are our contractors up to snuff?"

RELATIONSHIPS WITH PARTNERS

When you're a virtual company, your interactions with partners become more intentional, and they open the way for greater contributions and collaboration.

For example, we have a CPA on retainer who we call our "financial quarterback." He is a financial savant, and we are so lucky to have him. Years ago, he sold his prestigious CPA practice in Atlanta and is now in semi-retirement. He doesn't need the money, but he works for the love of it.

He works with a couple of choice companies and wealthy families doing financial consulting. He is very picky about who he works with...he deserves to be!

It's a real honor that he has chosen to work with BELAY. We can't pay him anywhere close to what other companies pay him, but he doesn't mind. To him, we are a unicorn. He has never seen anything like us...he was fascinated! He couldn't get over our virtual services, the fact that we have no hard costs, or that we don't have any major capital outlays, yet we're winning awards and are growing like crazy. We blew his mind and intrigued him.

When we started getting him involved in the leadership team, he said he would just phone in on our conference calls. He didn't have a webcam. He was old school. Imagine selling your CPA business after thirty years; everything he did was with paper and pencil! At BELAY, that just was not going to work for us. So, Shannon shipped him a webcam so he could really be a part of the whole experience. Now he loves being on video conferences. He loves the personal connection.

Through our video conferences, we've established a more meaningful relationship with him that we would not have been able to grow over the phone.

RELATIONSHIPS WITH EXTERNAL ORGANIZATIONS

Being virtual forces vendors to be more authentic when approaching us. Salespeople can't just drop by our office—because we don't have one! Our lack of office forces them to get creative to find ways to add value to our organization. It forces them to redefine their boundaries.

It also helps me filter out the people who I don't want to connect with. It shifts the power to me. In a typical venture capital firm or private equity group, interns are hired to cold call and email business owners all day long. Those kids have an MBA and are taught to say fancy words to get an owner on the hook to talk about their business and get them in some database somewhere. I know the game.

I get emails all the time that say, "Hey, we're going to be in Atlanta, we want to come by your office."

I tell them, "Sorry, I don't have one!" Crisis averted.

If a vendor reaches out to me and genuinely puts in the time to set up a meeting, I can choose to set up a Zoom call...or not. If I decide that I want to meet, I set up a Zoom call on my own time. Over that Zoom call, we can get a real, authentic conversation going.

Setting up partnerships over video conference is also more efficient and more cost effective. When using Zoom, I don't have to get on an airplane and lose three days of work to travel out west for a thirty-minute meeting.

Right now, we're setting up a partnership with an organization in Seattle. They are a great company that is growing very fast. They are similar to us in many ways, including my favorite way...they love Zoom, too! Every conversation we have with them is on Zoom. It works better for all of us as we get to know each other better.

We know we don't have to get on an airplane and meet in Kansas to have a great conversation about advancing our partnership with that company. We can just get on a web call, get used to each other, and then get to the deal points.

THE L-WORD: LIMITATIONS

I am here to be realistic. I'm not walking around with my head in the clouds; I know there are specific situations in which virtual just will not work. There are some businesses that absolutely need a brick-and-mortar space.

Retail has one such limitation. If you want to sell birdseed, you will need a retail space. But there is Amazon.

Hospitality (food service) is another. If you want to open a restaurant, you need a space for people to eat.

That is just the nature of their industries, but that is not to say that those industries aren't moving some aspects into a virtual world...

WE SEE AMAZING THINGS HAPPENING IN VIRTUAL WHERE WE NEVER THOUGHT POSSIBLE

Technology in general, and virtual environments specifically, can push businesses further than they thought possible. They can offer new and better services. While flying drones from Amazon Prime Air sound cool, here are some other current examples.

As I mentioned before, hospitals can now get patients on video calls with doctors inside a robot across the country to diagnose their symptoms and instruct the onsite medical teams about what they should do.

CloudFactory can chew through hours of audio files from courtroom proceedings in seconds.

Automattic, the founder of WordPress, enjoys a virtual staff of over four hundred people in forty-three countries and has a business valued in excess of one billion dollars.

McDonald's stock just recently hit an all-time high after announcing that it has begun the initiative to upgrade 2,500 of its restaurants to its "Experience of the Future" technology by 2018. The star feature of this upgrade: digital ordering kiosks!

Ally is taking their banking services to a new level by offering fantastic virtual experiences so that customers can connect.

Like grocery shopping? Kroger now has ClickList where you buy your goods online, they fulfill your order, and then place your groceries in your car trunk. Target just acquired Shipt for $550M to compete better and speed up delivery of goods to your doorstep.

Even hospitality is getting a shake-up! Cloud Kitchens out in Los Angeles is a new concept that offers chefs the ability to cook food for delivery only—no restaurant required. Just an iPad and a Wi-Fi connection are needed.

Alice Receptionist is a company that replaces greeters in office lobbies with virtual greeters through a software platform.

The list of current examples is endless! Yet we still have naysayers who don't connect the dots.

People are already working virtually, but they don't acknowledge it.

Sometimes we get prospects who tell me that they are intrigued by the whole "virtual assistant thing," but they don't think it could work for them. But just last night, they were FaceTiming with their mom who lives two thousand miles away. Just an hour ago, they were watching their stocks rise on their Vanguard app. Just a minute ago, they were checking their savings account balance on their Bank of America app. How is it that FaceTime is good enough to keep them close to their loved ones, but when it comes to work, they think video conference isn't good enough? How is it that they are okay with dealing with their personal assets on their iPhones, yet they are hesitant to hire an assistant that lives in the next state over? How is it that they're talking to me over the phone via a satellite that is orbiting over our heads in space, yet they don't think that they could close a deal over Zoom?

Let me tell you; their uncertainty is an act…they have already made the decision to go virtual. In fact, they are probably more virtual than they realize.

That excuse just does not work anymore.

FUTURE TECHNOLOGY...RIGHT AROUND THE CORNER?

I get a lot of questions from people in private equity, venture capital, and the media who ask me, "Are you afraid of Siri or AI?" My answer is always no.

"Why?" they ask. I tell them that Siri can't schedule a meeting for me without accidentally telling me the weather in Fargo, North Dakota. Siri does not think critically. Right now, Siri only possesses the ability to advance the ball through small tasks.

You still want your assistant to be able to critically think through a problem. Let's say that I missed my flight. Alexa isn't going to help me get a new one and then think through all of the things that I will have to fix: hotel reservations, meetings, car rentals, etc. Not to mention, on top of that, she isn't going to understand the subtleties of my own personal preferences. Alexa is not there yet. The need to have a critically thinking person to solve problems like that is decades off.

Businesses run because people can solve complex problems over and over and over again. AI just can't do that yet. AI is just "neat" right now. A lot of people say to me that it is so sexy, that it is the next big thing. It isn't. It's intriguing, but I'm jaded by it because I get asked the question all the time.

It's going to solve maybe some small, base layer problems or tasks, but it can't compensate for the human mind.

God made an incredible body and an unbelievable brain that is insanely complex. The idea that my brain could be replaced by something artificial is ridiculous to me. The variability that our brain accounts for the day-by-day, hour-by-hour irregularity of life...there is just no computer that could keep up.

MAKE THE LEAP

Now that you are visualizing how all of this could work, I'm going to take you through the practicalities of making the shift from physical to virtual...

CHAPTER 6

MAKE YOUR LANDLORD CRY

Leaders of organizations approach me and ask me if there is some way of knowing if their team could convert to remote or virtual. They want to know, "Are there symptoms to indicate my readiness?"

My answer is, "Yeah! There are symptoms."

To see how primed your company is to go virtual, take our easy Virtual Readiness Reckoning Quiz on our website at http://virtualculturebook.com/virtualreadiness.

LIFEWAY

Earlier in the book, I mentioned LifeWay and its CEO, Dr. Thom Rainer, and his quest to change the direction of the organization. He is doing something radical to a half-billion-dollar, 5,600-employee organization. I've never seen anyone do what he is doing.

I was honored to get the chance to sit down with Dr. Thom Rainer. I am now more honored to call Thom a friend. If you are in any way impressed with what my team and I have done at BELAY, get ready to have your socks blown off by Dr. Rainer and his team at LifeWay. I am so excited to be able to share his story.

Dr. Rainer came in as CEO of LifeWay eleven years ago. Before that, he was in banking, then the pastor of four churches, and then the dean of Southern Seminary in Louisville for twelve years.

LifeWay has been around since 1891, but Dr. Rainer has come in to shake things up in a big way: he's moving the organization into the twenty-first century in terms of technology, shifting to a hybrid workforce that includes remote and virtual employees.

I wondered what it was like coming into a 126-year-old organization and undertaking a move as great as this.

I wondered whether the organization was up for the task of evolving.

Dr. Rainer told me that LifeWay had "made some good transitions prior to [his] arrival, so it did not feel like a hundred-[plus-]year-old company." They were already doing well, and the organization was "postured where it needed to be" to continue that growth process. But of course, as Dr. Rainer says, in the world of technology, a year is like a lifetime. He knew it was his duty not to rest on his laurels, but rather to keep LifeWay plugging forward against the "headwinds...in order to move into the future."

Technology was certainly one of those headwinds. But he also said that one of the headwinds was the fact that all around him, he saw brick-and-mortar retail chains closing. Because half of LifeWay's revenue model was brick-and-mortar sales, and because LifeWay's biggest competitor is Amazon and their online sales are mammoth (Dr. Rainer has dubbed this the "Amazon Factor"), Dr. Rainer understood that he needed to act. He needed to act fast.

"What did you do?" I asked him.

"Well," he said, "I believe that success and failure in an organization is determined by putting the right people in the right places." He cited a favorite metaphor written by Jim Collins in *Good to Great*. Dr. Rainer said, "In fact, leaders of companies that go from good to great start not with 'where' but with 'who.' They start by getting the right people on the bus, the wrong people off the bus, and the right people in the right seats. And they stick with that discipline—first the people, then the direction—no matter how dire the circumstances."

If you transform the people for the better, the organizational structures will follow.

So, he decided that he was going to sell all of the 1.1 million square feet of real estate, move the organization to a smaller, more advanced office, hire on virtual contractors, and divide his current employees into three groups: a full-time on-site group, a group that would be 100 percent remote, and a group that would be a little of both.

You could say that not only was Dr. Rainer getting the right people in the right seats on the bus, but he was also lighting his old bus on fire and building a whole new bus.

I asked him what he said when his employees asked him, "Why?"

He said, "I gave them three words: Change or die." He wanted to steward them into the future.

If his employees weren't immediately convinced, he told them to look around and get their "heads out of the sand." Retail is closing down. Family Christian Stores, the largest Christian retailer in the world, just shut its doors. He told them to look at the struggles of secular stores like Radio Shack and Macy's. The list goes on.

"Once they did that," he said, "it was pretty convincing."

His primary why was convincing, but he also had three other why(s) that pushed him to start getting the right people in the right seats on the bus.

LifeWay's real estate situation with the cost of upkeep, and the "massive amounts of wasted space" was a major motivating factor.

Over one million square feet of prime space in downtown Nashville made up LifeWay's headquarters. They owned nine buildings on ten city blocks! They were the largest landowner in the entire city other than the government itself.

He said it didn't take a "brilliant person to realize that

something had to give. Yet, they continued to meet in the same place as always."

The buildings were a waste of space, and Dr. Rainer said they should have done away with them decades ago. But remember those entrenched and antiquated ideas leaders have about needing to see their employees to control them? LifeWay leaders were no exception: they fell prey to that same misconception. So, for decades, nobody wanted to make the decision to get rid of the wasted space because it would have been, in Dr. Rainer's words, "political business suicide."

Real estate aside, the commute into downtown Nashville was getting "extremely difficult" because of the insane growth of the city.

Lastly, there were cultural reasons why Dr. Rainer decided to take the leap. He said they "had over 90 percent of [our] employees in offices or cubicles, and collaboration is often difficult." For that reason, he wanted to update his workforce environment to "engender a greater collaboration."

So, with a compelling why in his pocket, Dr. Rainer set to work.

The first step he took was to study the move extensively.

He wanted to make sure this would be the best course of action for LifeWay. Once he confirmed his decision, his next step was to let his executive team know what he was planning.

I wondered what their reaction was. He said his leadership team saw the merit of it from the beginning. There were a couple members of the executive team who were averse to change and might have thought that Dr. Rainer was crazy, but he knew they would come around to the idea because change had to happen. Now, "everyone on [his] executive team understands [the change] and embraces it fully."

Once his team was on board, Dr. Rainer sought out expert advice. He wanted to get direction about how to proceed. He did not know in what way he should reorganize: What ratio of virtual to non-virtual employees would be best? What work environment should they be aiming to create? What would the future look like?

So, he engaged in a long consultation with a CEO of a premier office architectural firm in Nashville that specialize in space usage. The consultants were able to give him the clearest direction about what Dr. Rainer needed to create his vision. They jointly decided that they were going to construct a new, 25,000-square-foot office.

He said he would have never anticipated all of the components such a change would require. He was surprised at how granular the process had become. He even tasked a "furniture team" with deciding what type of furniture to have in their new office. He had a "historical team" to keep the historical memory alive as they "[moved] forward into the future."

Next, they brought in an external project manager through the consulting firm and appointed two internal project managers. His EVP was responsible for the physical changes, and the VP on his team was responsible for the cultural and communication changes. That VP formed an internal task force to deal with change management.

He said that his VP and EVP have been "instrumental in leading the entire employee force through this change management. [He's] rarely seen something carried [out] with excellence the way they have and the way that they've gotten the employees to not only simply buy into the idea, but to be a part of the ownership of the idea."

He, like me, is a delegator—he allows his employees to execute while he stays at the high level. This project was no exception; Dr. Rainer wanted his employees to buy into it, and he felt that involving his employees in the transition was the best way to go about that. Dr. Rainer and his leadership team appointed numerous employee teams so that everyone could feel involved in some way.

BUMPS IN THE ROAD

At one point, one of the employee-led change management teams came to Dr. Rainer with a dilemma. Through surveys, they had found that the majority of LifeWay employees had never worked in an environment that was not a cubicle farm. The team was worried about how the employees would react to the new office, which they had decided was going to be a new type of open-floor, collaborative space.

So, instead of asking questions...they searched for answers. They set up "LifeWay Lab" in the cafeteria of one of their old buildings. The Lab was designed to be a mock, look-alike portion of the office space that they would be moving to. There was not a single cubicle. Instead, there were giant tables, open meeting rooms, couches, and plenty of collaborative space. They wanted their employees to feel more connected to each other in a more agile and freeing environment.

They cycled their employee teams through two-week stints and asked for feedback. "What do you think about the furniture? How was the experience? Were there too many interruptions? What would you do differently?"

After each group had given their feedback, Dr. Rainer and his team implemented those suggestions for the next group that cycled in. Week after week, they iterated.

The employees responded "overwhelmingly positively." But, of course, there was not unanimity. "About 15 percent gave [us] a thumbs-down," said Dr. Rainer. Dr. Rainer's team asked why those employees were unhappy. They realized that for some, the reason they weren't happy was simply because they did not like change.

However, Dr. Rainer said that the employees did a "great job of adjusting and embracing" the change, but of course, change comes with challenges.

Communication was the largest such challenge. According to Dr. Rainer, "One of the biggest issues was communicating to our employees [about] the different groups" that they would be reorganizing in.

They had to explain that a few of the employees (namely C-Suite) would have offices. Another group would have assigned workplaces in the new office. The last group was "unassigned"—meaning they didn't have a place to come to at the new office, but they could work anywhere they wanted. Dr. Rainer and his team had to explain that employees were assigned to their group by role, not by hierarchy (except for the C-Suite). For example, if an employee was on the road often, they would group him in "unassigned." They determined the grouping methodically; they didn't guess. Each employee has a chip embedded into their badges so that they could record exactly where they were at all times and learn how often they were in the physical office.

"We needed to deliver this news [of the change] carefully." Dr. Rainer knew that if any one of his employees heard about the change for the first time in a big town hall meeting, they had failed. Those types of big conversations, Dr. Rainer believes, should happen in a private and personal environment. Otherwise, it would be a moral issue on LifeWay's part.

They wanted to make sure the message was proliferated from manager to employee directly and personally.

I asked him how he made sure that the message touched everyone. He told me there were multiple points of communication. "There is no such thing as too much redundancy in a major change like this."

They conducted departmental meetings, town halls, put out a multiplicity of digital and written communications, a newsletter, and talked about the change during the twice-a-month employee chapel. He went in front of his employees and communicated a lot, and so did the other executives. They had something called IntraLife (which is their internal internet), and they had a portal called "Ask Selma" in which any employee could send the VP in charge of change management a question at any time. They even put up a camera that showed a live feed of the construction of the new office (the much smaller new office). They wanted to create excitement about the progress of the move.

Dr. Rainer said there were so many points of communication that, if they counted all of them, it would be over a hundred ways. That was on purpose.

He says that when you're going through a massive change, there is no way you could over communicate. "The danger is always on the side of under communicating."

He also decided that they weren't going to take a lot of furniture, hardware, or technology with them. They are taking this opportunity to put the extra funds from downsizing and selling real estate into updating the whole organization.

He is providing a "constant flow" of training sessions to train employees on all of the new hardware and software that LifeWay would be converting to. He is moving a lot of his data to the cloud and housing his backup files on servers outside of Nashville. He also said they went nearly paperless. They knew that going into their new space, they wouldn't be taking paper files and file cabinets, so they would have to go fully digital.

VIRTUAL LIFEWAY

I asked more specifically about the move to a hybrid, virtual workforce where some employees were virtual, some were half, and some were on-site. In regard to the employee's feelings about working from home, Dr. Rainer said that it has been positive. A lot of their happiness stems from the relief that they feel over not having to endure a rigorous commute five days a week. Other employees have said they work better uninterrupted somewhere off-site.

I asked him if he took part in the virtual move himself. He said he has. For him personally, working from home "helps [his] productivity." He said he can't do any writing when he is in the office. When he needs to sit down and focus and dedicate four hours to some strategic issue, he does it better remotely because he gets uninterrupted blocks of time. He gets to focus a lot on writing—he is an author sixteen times over!

He said that if anyone had told him he was going to enact a work-from-home, or work-from-anywhere model, he would have said, "What is that?" Now he is a convinced man.

HERE'S OUR SHAMELESS PLUG

BELAY has been fortunate enough to be called to serve LifeWay in their endeavors. We have already provided Dr. Rainer and some members of his team with our virtual services.

Dr. Rainer had this to say about BELAY:

> What [BELAY] provides does not explain the totality of how much BELAY has helped us. What we get when we get with BELAY is not just a virtual workforce, but we get matched extremely well with workers. After working with them for a while, I see very clearly that yes, one of the strengths of working with BELAY is now we have virtual workers and it gives us a lot more flexibility, but it's not just virtual workers. It's the right caliber, quality, and fit of workers, and that's where, as a virtual placement organization, they seem to have an edge on almost everybody else. That's where they do the incredible job...matching you with the right virtual workers.

My relationship with BELAY is still in its early stages, but I can tell you this already: All of my expectations of what it would be like...have been exceeded. I have two assistants. I have an on-site assistant, and then I have a virtual assistant who I hired through BELAY. In regard to Jana, the virtual assistant, all of my expectations about what she could bring to the table and how much help she would provide me have been exceeded. She... gives me flexibility...and she is qualified and competent.

Dr. Rainer said that after looking to BELAY to match him with Jana, he has been able to accelerate his personal platform. He has a blog, a podcast, books, and other ways in which to connect with the evangelical world that he now can grow because he has more time and is more organized.

He says that as LifeWay continues to move toward a purer virtual working environment and look for more virtual workers, BELAY is his go-to.

WE'RE READY! NOW WHAT?

Ready to get on board with the virtual train? Ready to cancel your lease?

If you, dear, brave reader, were to hire BELAY to take you through this transition, this is what I would tell you to do...

STEPS TO GET EMPLOYEES WORKING IN A DIFFERENT WAY

You have to be intentional about the migration. Think about it: you will have employees who have worked in a traditional office space for twenty, thirty, maybe even forty years! That's a lot of time for a learned behavior to become ingrained. Now, all of a sudden, you are asking them to change that behavior by working from home? It's almost like the same kind of shock that a prisoner has when he is released from jail after twenty-some years and they have to go out in the real world. It is scary!

For that reason, you have to build that bridge by introducing them to their new world slowly. I recommend trial runs like the trial runs that Dr. Rainer conducted. One day a week for a couple of months before the transition, have your employees work from home or a coffee shop. Ramp those days up to two days a week, then three days a week, and so on.

Once you start the transition, you have to think about what tools are going to help employees stay productive outside an office. You have to make sure you have the technology ready to go when your employees open their computers while sitting at home. They must have high-speed internet access, a good webcam, an up-to-date computer, a quiet work environment, and most of all, they have to have the skills to hang in a web-based environment.

Once your employees have these tools, you need to make sure they know how to work with them.

ALRIGHT...STOP, COLLABORATE, AND SURVEY!

You want to make sure to create surveys that will help pinpoint your employees' hang-ups and struggles with the migration to working remotely.

Ask them what is difficult for them. Ask them what they are scared about. Ask them where they feel lost. Ask them if they are feeling anxious. Ask, ask, ask.

Let's say that in your survey, your employees frequently talk about how they are used to working on a desktop and in a desktop environment, and they don't want to go mobile. You're going to have to get your IT team together to figure out how to teach your employees about their new environments and to get your online environments ready for remote workers. If you find that those gaps are glaringly obvious, you've got to create a plan to fill those gaps.

SCHEDULE TIME FOR TRAINING

Scheduling time for training is so important. Not only does it get your employees ready, but it is also a wonderful time to deliver value face-to-face to reassure them of the migration. This is an opportunity to explore the not-so-obvious things your employees will need to know.

Let your employees practice in your new environment. Follow Dr. Rainier's advice.

IF YOU CAN AFFORD IT, APPOINT A FULL-TIME PROJECT MANAGER

If you can afford it, add a project manager to manage the migration. As Dr. Rainer said, there are more moving parts than you realize. There are many stakeholders involved, but you need someone who will be there pushing forward every day. That is why it is important to appoint someone who will be responsible for it all early on. You need someone to be accountable because, otherwise, the migration can drag out if you don't...which could mean problems for your business.

MAKE SURE TO CAST THE VISION OF A COMPELLING WHY

Employees can see right through most leaders, so a leader must make sure that his why is compelling. The why needs to be more than just the owner saying, "I'd love to work on my back deck!"

It has to be more than that. It has to be about saving money, reinvesting that money to grow the business, and allowing greater personal and professional flexibility for the employees so they can take their lives back. It cannot just be all about the CEO.

The owner or CEO must communicate the why over and over again. This should be communicated up to, throughout, and after the migration. As we learned with LifeWay, this is massively important.

I work at casting vision and communicating my why every chance I get, and I feel like my employees appreciate it. I know I am winning at casting vision when my employees lovingly mock me about what I say. When this happens, I know that my vision is getting through to them. If you plan to migrate to a virtual workplace, you must master vision casting. Your why must be gravitating and crystal clear.

CONCLUSION

WORKPLACE APOCALYPSE

———

Shannon and I have been ahead of the curve for a long time with regards to creating and enjoying a virtual culture. We are running a seven-year-old business that is still considered to be on the cutting edge of workplace innovation. We have had a vision for the type of flexible, virtual workplace we've always desired—even when we faced major headwinds at times.

Now, we are looking toward the future...again.

WHAT THE FUTURE HOLDS

My prediction: in twenty years, almost all employees will

be contractors, with most of them working in a remote/ virtual capacity. Cubicles will be a relic of times past. It won't be about the hours you worked; it'll be about the results you produced.

Earlier in this book, I referenced Accenture's prediction that by 2020, 43 percent of the workforce will be freelance. Accenture labeled this group, "the liquid workforce." Well, 2020 is just around the corner. If that doesn't sound an alarm in your head as an employer, then nothing will. You've got to realize: it is coming. It's coming like a tsunami swelling beyond your eye's horizon. I believe it is here to stay in a very permanent way.

Why?

People are ruined once they get a taste of working from home. They will not go back into an office. End of story. They might go back in the office to take a higher-paying job, but they will end up hating it and quit. We see it all the time. Money and benefits are not greater than employee flexibility.

I see this every day, and not just with front-line employees... highly paid people are moving this way, too. A friend of ours is a senior principal at a big-time business management consultancy. He lives in Los Angeles, but his office is in San Francisco. He flies back and forth every week. But more and more, he is pushing back. He is telling his employer that they can either allow him to work from home or sweeten his paycheck. He told his boss that he has young kids and wants to be home more. He has shown them that he is actually more productive working from home. He's been bitten by the bug, and he is not willing to go back. Employers: you are now on notice.

I see this all the time. I see employees who, instead of negotiating for raises, are asking for more flex time, aka work-from-home days.

Any CEO of a company who is reading this and doesn't believe the process has begun needs to raise their head and look out on the horizon. They're going to have to realize they will need to make decisions about how to create an environment where a certain percentage of their talent is remote and demands workplace flexibility.

They have to start now because it's going to be a work-place apocalypse.

TECHNOLOGY: THE ULTIMATE WINGMAN

Advancements in technology enhance the working relationship, especially around the communication aspects of running a business. Part of the reason BELAY is still alive today is that high-speed internet access is pervasive and consistent throughout the country—at least more so than it was ten years ago.

A second technological advancement that enabled BELAY to succeed is superior web-based technology. Every year, web-based applications become more advanced, and millions of dollars are pumped into them to ensure their security and reliability. This permits our employees to be mobile. This is obviously huge for us! Our employees aren't tethered to slow desktop environments that keep them chained to their desks.

ENTREPRENEUR OPPORTUNITY!

There are a handful of legitimate workplace personality assessments. Myers-Briggs, DiSC, Enneagram, and the Kolbe are just a few. These tests are all based on how people interact face-to-face. But there is an opportunity for someone to create a new personality assessment for virtual or remote employees who are not working face-to-face. Virtual environments require different characteristics and skills than non-virtual environments.

A RADICAL SHIFT IN CORPORATE OFFICE SPACE

Think about all of the commercial real estate—office space—in our country that will be empty. Certainly, if almost all of the working population will be remote by 2037, can you imagine how much corporate real estate space will be abandoned? All of those huge, bland corporate office buildings will be carcasses.

I already see it happening. LifeWay abandoned 1.1 million square feet. I can drive within a half a mile perimeter around my house and see two abandoned office complexes in metro Atlanta.

What is going to happen to this space? What will we do about it? Are we going to demolish it and replace it with parks? Are we going to have non-profits come in and turn empty buildings into homeless shelters? We have an opportunity to turn this once-solemn place into a place that can benefit the people in our country in a new and different way.

Whole industries will have to come face-to-face with their demise. Maintenance companies who care for buildings will die. Ancillary industries that support corporate real estate will die. Architects will have to find other types of structures to design.

Even those industries that you can't imagine not being in a physical space, like higher education, are changing. More and more, professors are teaching their classes from their home offices.

HUMAN RESOURCE CHANGES AND ORGANIZATION CHALLENGES

Human Resources needs to get ahead of the curve and start thinking through how employees' rights will look once they work from home. They will also have to start thinking about how to build a culture and keep people emotionally connected to a company in a virtual world.

We're fortunate at BELAY because we've had the ability to think through these problems from a blank slate. I don't know how that will look for people who have to change an already existing structure and culture.

Regardless, leaders must have a serious conversation. There will be new legal precedents, regulatory modifications coming from the government, new protections for people working from home, corporate liability shifts, conversations about data ownership, and previously unexplored privacy concerns.

CONTINUE YOUR EDUCATION

I want to recommend some other great resources to further your virtual education. These are resources that have spoken to me on my journey.

1. *Remote: Office Not Required* by Jason Fried and David Heinemeier Hansson
2. *Rework* by Jason Fried and David Heinemeier Hansson
3. *A Manager's Guide to Virtual Teams* by Yael Zofi
4. *The Virtual Assistant Solution: Come up for Air, Offload the Work You Hate, and Focus on What You Do Best* by Michael Hyatt
5. *Virtual Freedom: How to Work with Your Virtual Staff to Buy More Time, Become More Productive, and Build Your Dream Business* by Chris Ducker
6. *The 4-Hour Work Week* by Tim Ferriss

TAKE ACTION

If the oncoming workplace apocalypse scares you, you can find a safe harbor on our blog https://belaysolutions.com/blog/. We cover meaningful and insightful solutions to everyday problems. Topics range from how to deal with an ineffective virtual manager to what to do if you have been hacked to a day in the life of a virtual worker to general conversations on virtual workforces.

On our website, https://belaysolutions.com, we have a lot of free resources available for download because we care about offering up great advice. Grab these free resources, and if you are interested, reach out to us.

When exploring our website, it is important to remember that BELAY's services are not intuitive. Our services mandate a conversation...a dialogue. That's why we have a team of people called Solutions Consultants who you can connect with to figure out your needs and to see if we are a good fit.

The truth is, we're qualifying you as much as you're qualifying us. I know it sounds salesy, but it's the truth.

CHANGE YOUR MINDSET, CHANGE YOUR FUTURE

I wish I could have captured every negative comment I have heard in the past seven years of building this business.

"You can't do this. It is impossible."

"This is a fad."

"You can't build a completely virtual company. It's never been done before."

"You're not a legitimate business if you are all virtual."

"As the economy improves, everyone will be back in the office."

The more people told me I couldn't, the more I believed I could.

And now we have done it. Not only did we prove the naysayers wrong, but we proved them wrong in a big way. People who were once critics have turned a corner. Some even want to be a part of the company now.

My experience has not been unique. There are leaders out there who have also been told that they can't. But they found ways against the odds and against all doubt. These are the leaders who fight to see the future clearly and who know that they need to embrace it.

They, like me, recognize that the tide is going to turn. The earthquake is going to hit. The ocean is going to boil. Pick whatever apocalyptic analogy you like best. It doesn't matter; they're all relevant.

Bottom line: we see a future where, one day, employees are just going to say, "I'm done."

They are going to get up from their desks and walk away from companies that frankly just don't get that employee flexibility (personally and professionally) is greater than money or benefits.

Where are they going to go? They are going to come to companies that offer them fair pay, flexibility, a meaningful why, more time with their families, a highly limited commute, and a life. For most, money won't be why they walk.

BELAY SAYS YES TO VIRTUAL, AND SO DO OUR CLIENTS

Early on, I was on the phone with someone who was looking to hire out BELAY's services. He liked me, and we had some fun conversations, so he asked if he could meet me in person to sign the final contract.

My initial reaction was, "Sure!" I mean, I was a salesman—meeting my clients in person was what I did for most of my career. It was natural for me. But I resisted the initial urge and challenged my own thinking.

I decided to take a leap.

I said, "With all due respect, if I have to come to see you, then I have just completely defeated the purpose of this service and my business."

He paused. I waited to hear how this would land with him. Then he started cracking up. He said, "All right, you're right! I'll sign. Send the contract." He happily signed the contract that day.

This was an "aha" moment that got me thinking. "What else can we do if we don't have to physically be next to people to execute results?" That is the shift in thinking that can occur for other leaders and owners. That shift is happening. There is just so much that can get done when you decide you don't need to do everything in person.

The worker of tomorrow is not the worker of today.

They're longing for a virtual culture.

ABOUT THE AUTHOR

 **BRYAN MILES** is CEO and Co-Founder of BELAY, alongside his wife Shannon. A leading US-based, virtual solutions company, BELAY has over six hundred team members—all working from home, remotely. Without an office, BELAY has graced the Inc. 5000 list three times and was awarded the number one spot in *Entrepreneur Magazine*'s rankings for Best Company Culture. BELAY provides virtual assistants, bookkeeping, copywriting, and webmaster services to leaders and fast-paced organizations. BELAY's services equip leaders and organizations with the ability to climb higher when and where they need it most. BELAY's vision is to help others achieve their vision.

Bryan and Shannon live with their two children, Harper and Rainey, in Atlanta. Practicing what he preaches, Bryan spends his days virtually running his company from his porch in Georgia, from the mountains in Jackson Hole, or from the beaches in the panhandle of Florida.